Previous page   'Devonshire butter', a photograph by A. W. Searley, c. 1900. Farmers' wives in the West Country often used to make butter, as here, by simply stirring and beating clotted cream.

MAKING CHEESES

There is increasing interest today in home-produced food: people all over the country are growing their own vegetables, brewing their own beer and wine, baking their own bread. This book describes how it is also possible to make cheese at home, without any very complicated equipment or special premises. Susan Ogilvy explains in detail the techniques for making hard, semi-hard and soft cheeses. She gives step-by-step instructions for many delicious delicacies: fresh milk cheese, cream cheese, traditional soft cheeses such as Crowdie, Colwick and Cambridge, the larger Smallholder cheese and the Small Cheshire. She also describes how you can make other dairy products at home, from yoghurt and butter to fresh clotted cream.

Although the book will obviously interest those such as farmers' wives who have a ready supply of milk, and people who are aiming at self-sufficiency, it has been written specifically with non-specialists in mind, ordinary housewives and others who obtain their milk from the local dairy roundsman.

Home-produced cheese has a wholesome good taste that no shop product can imitate. By making cheese at home, you will not only save money but will enjoy a fascinating and very satisfying craft, with a delicious and nutritious end-product.

Overleaf *A photograph of some of the cheeses described in this book*

Making Cheeses

Susan Ogilvy

B. T. Batsford Ltd London

© Susan Ogilvy 1976
First published 1976
Second impression 1977

ISBN 0 7134 3168 7

Filmset by Servis Filmsetting Ltd, Manchester
Printed in Great Britain by Morrison & Gibb Ltd, Edinburgh
for the Publishers B. T. Batsford Ltd,
4 Fitzhardinge Street London W1H 0AH

Contents

ACKNOWLEDGMENT

The Author would like to thank the following people for the valuable help and advice they provided in the writing of this book: R. Osborne of the Milk Marketing Board; J. W. Hughes and Miss D. F. Williams of ADAS, Ministry of Agriculture, Fisheries and Food; B. A. Galloway of the Somerset College of Agriculture and Horticulture; Miss M. Johnston of Lackham College of Agriculture, Wiltshire; A. L. Walker of the West of Scotland Agricultural College; Mrs L. Hetherington of the British Goat Society; and the many readers of *Farmers Weekly* who wrote to tell her of their own experiences in cheesemaking.

The following books and leaflets were particularly useful: *Home Made Cheeses,* A 'Farm Woman's Library' Book, Hulton Press, 1957; *The Backyard Dairy Book*, published by Whole Earth Tools, 1972; *The Story of Cheesemaking in Britain*, by V. Cheke, Routledge and Kegan Paul, 1959; *Dictionary of Dairying,* by J. G. Davis, Leonard Hill, 1965; *Dairy Work for Goatkeepers*, published by the British Goat Society, 1973; *A Handbook of Dairy Foods*, issued by the National Dairy Council; *Cooking with Yoghurt, Cultured Cream and Soft Cheese,* by Bee Nilson, Pelham Books, 1973; and the advisory leaflets issued by the Ministry of Agriculture, Fisheries and Food: *Soft Cheese, Cream Cheese, Cream, Clotted Cream* and *Starters for Cheesemaking.*

The Author and Publishers would also like to thank John Walters for the drawings. The frontispiece photograph was taken by Colin Futcher.

Note for American readers
The American equivalent for the British
   Single Cream is Light Cream
   Double Cream is Heavy Cream
   Sultanas is Raisins

An Introduction to Cheesemaking 1

THE HISTORICAL BACKGROUND

Cheesemaking is an ancient craft – one that goes right back to the
beginnings of civilization. The first cheeses were probably made by early
nomadic tribes on the borders of Europe and Asia. These tribesmen knew
that if a food was dried it was easier to carry and was also preserved for
longer in an edible condition. Milk could be partially dried by being left
in a shallow vessel to evaporate in the sun. The warmth caused the milk
to sour and an acid-curd cheese was formed. Perhaps rennet-curd cheese
was later discovered when milk was carried by tribesmen in bags made
from animals' stomachs.

    Cheese was a favourite food of the Ancient Greeks and Romans, and
various ways of making it developed. Its nutritional value was recognized
too, for in Sparta wrestlers training for the Games had to include it in
their diet, and the Roman legions used to carry cheese as an essential food
ration on their marches. The Romans also influenced the development of
cheesemaking in Britain; during their occupation cheese became a popular
food. A description of cheesemaking written at the time shows that they
had a good understanding of hygiene, the use of rennet, and the draining,
salting and storing of cheese. The general methods used then changed
little over the years until the nineteenth century.

    The early cheeses were of a soft type; gradually ways of making
harder cheese which kept longer were developed. Methods were handed
down from generation to generation, mainly by word of mouth. The ways
to obtain the best results were learned only by trial and error, and important factors such as the development of acidity were little understood. It

9

was not until the nineteenth century that scientific principles were applied to cheesemaking: the different varieties were classified and methods were standardized for making them. The variety of cheese came to be identified by the name of the region in which it was made or marketed. Today comparatively few of the varieties remain; some are extinct and others have merged. On pages 13–16 there are details of the main sorts of cheese available in this country today.

THE PRINCIPLES OF CHEESEMAKING

Milk is a unique food. At times, because so many different products can be made from it, it seems almost to be endowed with magic properties. Before beginning to make cheese from milk it is important to understand a few of the principles involved, and how the properties of milk make cheesemaking possible.

Two properties of milk are important in cheesemaking: (i) liquid milk can clot to form a solid curd, and (ii) milk can sour and become more acid.

Milk owes its ability to clot to the presence of a protein called casein; casein precipitates – separates into a solid – when rennet is added, or when the milk turns very acid. When this happens the milk becomes junket-like in consistency, forming a curd in which liquid whey is held, a process known as coagulation or clotting.

Rennet is a substance found in the stomach of young mammals which enables the milk – their first food – to form a clot so that it can be easily digested. This is why the milk clotted when the early tribesmen carried it in bags made from animals' stomachs. Since then man has extracted the rennet and used it to make cheeses and junket.

Rennet works best when the milk is warm and contains soluble calcium. Milk naturally contains calcium in a soluble form, but if it is boiled or heated to a high temperature this calcium becomes insoluble, and the rennet will not work. This explains why you cannot use boiled, sterilized or ultra-heat-treated ('long-life') milk to make junket or cheese.

Rennet also works best when the milk has soured and is slightly acid. Milk owes its ability to sour to the presence of lactose or milk sugar. Lactose can be changed to lactic acid by certain bacteria, and this increases the acidity of the milk. Lactic acid-producing bacteria use the lactose for growth and ferment it to lactic acid. They are naturally present in raw untreated milk and cause normal souring when this milk is kept in warm conditions for some time. However, they are not present in sufficient quantity in pasteurized milk.

Most milk now sold in the UK undergoes pasteurization, a heat treatment which destroys all the disease-causing organisms and ensures that the milk is absolutely safe to drink. Pasteurization also kills most of the lactic acid-producing bacteria present in the milk, so improving its keeping quality. Therefore, with pasteurized milk, a special culture of lactic acid bacteria has to be used to start the souring process. The use of a culture also helps to ensure that the growth of bacteria is carefully controlled. The cultures used in cheesemaking are known as cheese 'starters'.

Rennet curd forms the basis of most hard and soft cheeses. But, as mentioned previously, the milk protein can be precipitated solely by high acidity (the acidity needed is much greater than that required in order for rennet to work). In such cases a bacterial culture is again used for the production of acidity, and the resulting acid curd is the basis of acid-curd cheese, yoghurt and other cultured milk products.

When the milk has been coagulated either by the rennet or by high acidity, the resulting curd is treated in various ways – depending on the type of cheese being made – in order to release the whey. Whey consists mostly of water and lactose; the fat and other constituents of milk remain caught in the curd with the protein.

Acidity continues to develop throughout cheesemaking and is a vital part of the process, particularly (as will be seen) in the making of hard cheese. It helps to give the finished cheese its flavour, and also checks the growth of other organisms which could be harmful, thereby acting as a preservative.

THE MANUFACTURE OF HARD CHEESES

There are many hundreds of varieties of cheese made throughout the world, but these varieties can be grouped into various types according to their method of manufacture and ripening, and their physical properties. In the UK most of our national cheeses are of the hard pressed type such as Cheddar or Cheshire. So we will discuss first the basic steps involved in the making of a typical hard cheese.

Certain fundamental steps are the same for almost all hard cheeses, and only small changes in these individual processes produce the different varieties. The flavour and texture of the finished cheese are determined by slight differences in times and temperatures, in the weight of pressing and the length of maturing.

Souring or ripening the milk   Starter culture is added to warm milk in large cheese vats. The milk is left for about 45 minutes to sour or ripen. The development of acidity at a steady rate is very important in the making of hard cheese and must be carefully controlled throughout the process in order to produce a good cheese. The development of acidity at various stages can be judged by physical changes in the curd, and these are learned only by experience. However now the commercial cheesemaker can also measure the acidity by chemical tests; this is a much surer method. The use of a reliable starter culture helps to ensure the development of acidity at a steady rate.

Renneting   Next the milk is heated to about 85°–95°F (29°–35°C), and rennet is gently stirred in. If the cheese is to be red, colouring is added before renneting. The milk is left for about 45 minutes to coagulate.

Cutting the curd   When the curd is firm – like a solid junket – it is ready for cutting. Horizontal and vertical bladed knives are passed through the curd to cut it into pea-sized cubes and free much of the whey which is held in the curd.

Scalding the curd   The curd pieces floating in the whey are heated slowly to about 100°F (38°C) over a period of about an hour. They are stirred continuously. This 'scalding' causes the curd pieces to shrink and helps to release still more whey. The continued development of acidity in the curd has a similar effect, and the rate of this development is important. If the curd develops acidity too fast, instead of forming firm and resilient pieces it becomes an unmanageable mass and pulls out in slimy wet strings. If the acidity is too low the curd will remain soft and sweet and will retain moisture, so that the cheese will spoil later by releasing moisture after a few weeks. The cheesemaker must keep a proper balance between the acidity and the moisture content of the curd by adjusting the degree and length of scalding and whey drainage. If the curd is developing acidity too fast it must be drained of whey more quickly by scalding it to a higher temperature over a shorter time; if the curd is 'working slowly' slow scalding to a lower temperature will result in slower whey drainage.

Draining the whey   After scalding the curd settles, and the whey is run off. As the curd settles it consolidates and shrinks. It is cut into blocks which are piled, turned and repiled on each side of the cheese vat leaving a drainage channel for the whey. During this draining period the curd consolidates and shrinks further, and the acidity increases. The curd changes in texture.

Milling and salting the curd   The curd is milled – broken up into small pieces – and salt is added and well mixed in. This salt helps to preserve the finished cheese and to bring out its flavour.

Moulding and pressing the curd   The curd is next packed into moulds and pressed for varying lengths of time and under varying pressures depending on the variety of cheese. The cheese may be bandaged, and covered with wax or sprayed with hot water to ensure that it keeps properly.

Maturing the cheese   Finally the finished cheese is placed in a special room to ripen and slowly mature. This room is kept at a temperature of 50°F (10°C), with a relative humidity of 80–90 per cent. The steady temperature ensures even ripening, and the correct humidity prevents shrinkage of the cheese due to evaporation. The cheese is turned every day at first and then less frequently later. During ripening various chemical changes occur which provide the flavour and texture of mature cheese. These result from the action of bacteria and enzymes in the curd. The bacteria in the 'starter' culture contribute to the process. Enzymes present in the rennet continue slowly to break down the protein, making it more digestible and the cheese mellow. The cheese becomes firm and the rind more definite.

Types of hard cheese

Only a few of the many English hard cheeses are widely available now, but these are all quite distinctive in taste, colour and texture. Cheddar, Cheshire, Derby, Double Gloucester and Leicester are hard pressed, so they have a relatively low moisture content and can be left to mature for a longer time to achieve their full flavour. There is nothing to beat an English Cheddar if it has been well matured. It needs at least 3 months; a good Cheddar is usually ripe at 6 months and mellow at 9 months.

Lancashire, Caerphilly and Wensleydale are semi-hard cheeses. As they are only lightly pressed they are moister and quicker to ripen than the hard pressed varieties. Continental hard and semi-hard cheeses include Edam and Gouda, Gruyère, Emmental and Parmesan.

The characteristic blue veining in Blue Stilton (and other 'blue' cheeses) is caused by a harmless mould which grows in the air spaces and cracks in the curd. The curd is not pressed but packed loosely into hoops. Aeration may be increased by piercing the curd with wires. Again Stilton is best eaten when fully ripe, not less than 6 months and preferably 9 months after it has been made.

SOFT CHEESES

A number of different types of cheese can be classified as soft cheeses; they are characterized by their small size and their comparatively high moisture content. The curd is drained slowly without pressure, by gravity, and therefore has a high moisture content compared to the pressed varieties and is quicker to ripen.

True soft cheese

This is made from fresh milk which is coagulated by rennet. The development of acidity is not as crucial as it is in the making of hard cheese, and a softer curd is formed. However starter is usually added just before the rennet and gives a clean, acid flavour to the resulting cheese. The rennet takes longer to set the milk because there is no acid development at this stage; the acidity develops later during the slow whey draining process. The curd is ladled into traditional moulds or hung up in muslin bags and allowed to drain slowly for up to several days.

At one time there were many English soft cheeses but only a few have survived. These are usually eaten in a fresh or unripened state at a few days old. In European countries soft cheeses are very popular and there are a wealth of different varieties. Many of these – the well known Camembert and Brie cheeses are examples – are ripened. As we have seen, the slow ripening of a hard pressed cheese is due to the action of bacteria in the low-moisture curd; in soft cheeses, surface moulds are the major agents and grow very quickly on the moist, acid surface. The moulds

14

secrete certain enzymes which break down or digest the curd and produce the characteristic texture and strong flavour. The ripening proceeds towards the centre until there is a soft creamy mass throughout. You can tell the ripeness of a soft cheese by pressing the middle and feeling the softness at the centre.

Ripening soft cheeses require a warm atmosphere which will encourage the growth of moulds. The desired moulds may be present in the atmosphere of the particular cheese factory, or the curd may be sprayed or inoculated with an appropriate culture.

Acid-curd cheese

Acid-curd cheese is another type of soft cheese although not a true one, since rennet is not used to coagulate the milk. Acid-curd cheese is formed solely by the action of lactic acid upon the casein. This acid curdling is a completely different from rennet coagulation, and gives a curd of high acidity, quick drainage properties and granular texture. The curd is usually drained in a muslin bag. The cheese will not ripen on storage and should be eaten when very fresh. Lactic cheese is an example of an acid-curd cheese.

A note of warning is needed here. In the past acid-curd cheese was traditionally made from milk which had gone sour. However, this was raw milk which had soured 'normally'. It is not advisable to use pasteurized milk which has soured or gone off for cheesemaking or in cooking. Pasteurized milk keeps for longer because nearly all the lactic acid bacteria are destroyed by the heat treatment. If it does go 'off', this may be caused by the growth of other bacteria which could be harmful. It is always wiser to throw such milk away.

Cottage cheese

This is made from skimmed milk from which the cream has been separated. Traditional British cottage cheese, such as Crowdie, is not the same as the American cottage cheese you can buy in a carton. The American version is made from skimmed milk coagulated by acid; the curd is washed several times to produce the characteristic separate particles.

Cream cheeses

Cream cheeses are not really true cheeses since they are made from gravity-drained cream. They have a rather granular, spreadable texture, a rich, creamy, mildly acid flavour, and can be moulded into various shapes and sizes.

THE NUTRITIONAL VALUE OF CHEESE

Cheese has an excellent nutritional value; it is one of the best and most economical protein foods, and a very good source of calcium. It is therefore an important food for children, especially if they don't drink much milk. But cheese can play an essential part in the diet of the whole family, both young and old. It is extremely versatile and can be eaten at any meal of the day, including breakfast, or as a snack, cooked or raw. It goes well with both sweet and savoury foods, as the protein in the main course, or as part of the dessert.

So make sure there is plenty of cheese in the house, and GOOD CHEESEMAKING!

A NOTE ON DAIRY HYGIENE

Before starting to make cheese it is a good idea to be aware of the dangers which may arise unless proper care is taken. Because milk is such a good food it is also an ideal medium for the growth of bacteria and other micro-organisms. Special attention must therefore be paid to ensure that the milk and utensils used are thoroughly clean, and prevent any chance of contamination. Not only will the taste and appearance of the products be spoiled, but the growth of harmful bacteria could well cause food poisoning.

To help avoid these dangers read particularly carefully the sections on the heat treatment of milk and its subsequent cooling (pages 26–7), the sterilization and care of the utensils and premises used (pages 24–5), and the cultivation of a reliable cheese starter (page 29).

But remember, if in doubt as to the wholesomeness of your produce, throw it away!

Equipment 2

EQUIPMENT NEEDED FOR MAKING SOFT CHEESE

The equipment needed for making soft cheese is relatively simple, and much of it can be improvised from ordinary kitchen utensils. It is worth spending a bit more on those articles that you do buy to make sure that they are of good quality. A list of suppliers is given in the appendix on pages 83–4.

You will need the following:

Thermometer
A proper dairy thermometer which floats on the surface of the liquid is best. If you have difficulty in obtaining this an ordinary jam-making thermometer can be used, but you will have to hold it in the liquid. It must be graduated to 220°F (104°C).

Room thermometer
This is useful for checking the temperature of the area where you make cheese, incubate starter or store the maturing cheese. Maintenance of the correct temperature is important. This thermometer can be obtained quite cheaply from a chemist.

Measuring jug
A 2-pint measuring jug is useful to measure out the necessary quantities of milk or cream.

17

1. Some equipment for cheesemaking

Mixing bowls

An assortment of 1-pint, 2-pint and 4-pint capacity bowls are required to hold the milk. The size needed depends on the type of cheese being made and the quantity of milk involved. Ordinary Pyrex mixing bowls are suitable, but stainless steel bowls can also be obtained.

Buckets

For larger quantities of milk use a 2-gallon capacity bucket. Stainless steel is best – never use galvanized iron or zinc, or aluminium, as these corrode. There is a strong plastic dairy bucket available which will withstand most of the temperatures used, is easy to sterilize and cheaper than stainless steel.

Water bath

The milk should nearly always be heated indirectly, in a water bath. The water bath can be an ordinary saucepan provided it is larger than the bowl containing the milk. Larger bowls or buckets can be stood in a sink of hot water – you can top up the water in the sink with more hot water from the tap.

Cheese cloths

These are squares of cloth used for draining the curd. You can make them yourself from good quality butter muslin bought from any dress fabric shop. They should be about 18 inches to 2 feet square and of double thickness. You will also need some odd pieces of string to tie and hang up the muslin draining bags.

Spoons, ladles and knives

A long handled spoon is needed for stirring the milk; a tablespoon and a teaspoon for measuring cheese starter and rennet; a perforated spoon and a soup-type ladle for ladling curd; a knife with a long blade for cutting the curd. Ordinary kitchen utensils are quite sufficient, but they should be of stainless steel. A set of plastic measuring spoons – $\frac{1}{4}$, $\frac{1}{2}$, 1 teaspoon, and 1 tablespoon – will be useful for measuring small quantities.

A plastic or stainless steel colander

This makes the task of placing the curd in the cheese cloth much easier. The colander can be lined with cheese cloth, placed over a bowl and then the curd can be spooned into it.

Moulds

These can be of various types. Traditionally the different soft cheeses were each made in their own type of mould (see the section on making soft cheeses), but unfortunately only the Coulommiers hoops (illustration 13 page 43) can still be obtained. You can improvise quite successfully, however, with round or square bottomless cake tins, or with large cocoa tins from which the base has been cut or which have holes pierced in the side (illustration 2). The tins which contain ground coffee are also suitable. Punch holes from the inside of the tin outwards so that there are no jagged edges inside to tear the cheese. You will find that the moulds made from cocoa or coffee tins have a relatively short life as they do corrode with use, and should be replaced as necessary.

19

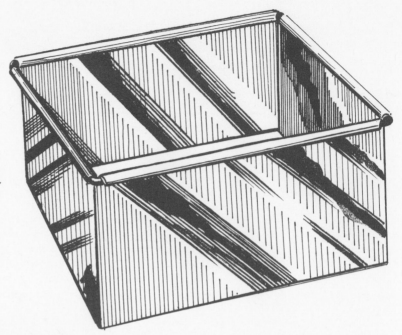

Square cake
tin with the
base removed

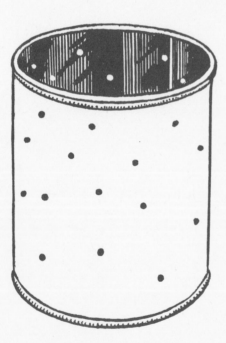

Cocoa tin with
the base removed
and holes
pierced in
the side

2. Improvised moulds

Cheese boards

These are used for placing the moulds on while the cheese is draining. They should be of hard, well-seasoned wood, about ½ inch thick. The actual size will depend on the size and number of moulds you are using. For example boards 13 inches by 7 inches will hold two Coulommiers moulds or two 6-inch square tins for Cambridge cheese; boards 7 by 7 inches will hold one Coulommiers mould or one Cambridge mould at a time. You can ask a do-it-yourself husband to make these for you, or a local wood merchant may be prepared to cut the wood to the right size. You will need two boards of each size.

Straw mats

These are used on the boards for drainage purposes. They should be of the same length and width as the boards. Straw mats in use now are made of pulped wood strips; originally they were made by threading together rye straws. Unfortunately these mats can no longer be bought, but you can improvise with straw table mats cut down to the right size. If you cannot obtain suitable straw mats, folded cheese cloths can be used.

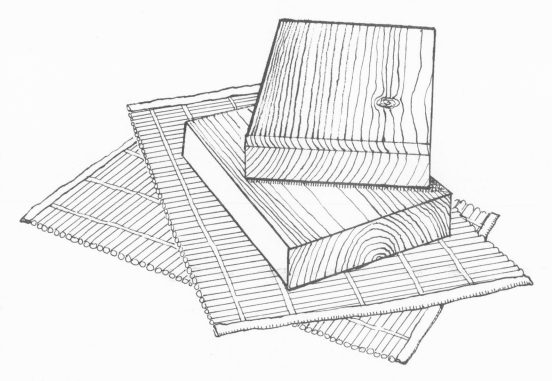

3. Straw mats and cheese boards

Container for collecting the whey
When making soft cheese in moulds there is a continuous flow of whey, and a container in which the cheese board can be placed is needed to collect the liquid. A roasting tin can be used to take longer cheese boards.

Scales
These are useful for weighing the finished curd. Ordinary kitchen scales can be used.

Small screw-cap glass bottles for starter recultivation
See the section on cheese starter, pages 29–37.

EQUIPMENT NEEDED FOR SEMI-HARD CHEESE

You will need much of the same equipment required for making soft cheese:
a dairy thermometer; a room thermometer; a measuring jug;
a 2–3 gallon bucket for making cheese; a spare bucket for collecting whey;
cheese cloths; a teaspoon, tablespoon, or measuring spoons,
long handled spoon, long bladed knife; starter bottles.
In addition you will need:

A cheese mould and press
You may be able to obtain a proper cheese press secondhand (illustration 4). This takes the curd from 6–7 gallons of milk. Unfortunately it is now difficult to buy one new, but again you can improvise with a cake tin, wooden follower and weights (illustration 5). A 6-inch diameter cake tin punched with holes would be most suitable; this takes the curd from 2 gallons of milk. The wooden follower which presses the cheese down the mould should be made of hard, well-seasoned wood, just smaller than the cake tin in diameter and about 1–2 inches thick. A local wood merchant may be willing to make this for you. The weights are then placed on top of the follower – building bricks or other similar weights can be used; the actual weight needed will depend on the variety of cheese being made. (I was lucky to find a door weight of 30 lbs which is ideal for pressing Smallholder cheese.)

A tin for collecting the whey as the cheese is pressed
A small flan tin in which the cheese mould can be placed will be sufficient as most of the whey will have been released during previous processes.

Butter muslin for making the cheese bandage

4. A cheese press

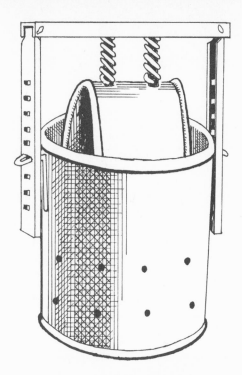

5. An improvised cheese press

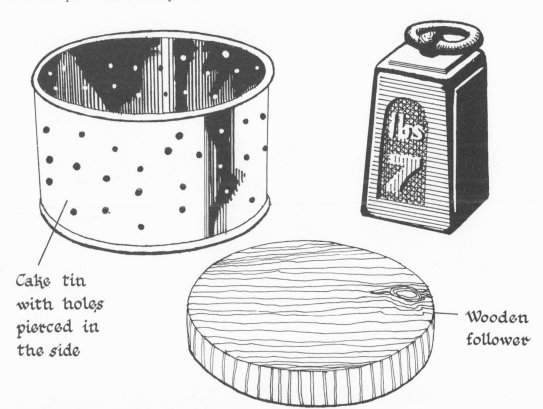

Cake tin
with holes
pierced in
the side

Wooden
follower

PREMISES

If you live on a farm you may have a scullery, large larder, suitable
outhouse or even a dairy that you can adapt into a special cheesemaking
room. However, if you have no other suitable room, the kitchen will do
well. The room chosen must first of all be cleaned very thoroughly, and
subsequently be kept very clean. Contamination of the milk or curd could
lead to serious defects in the cheese.

The room temperature should range from 65°–70°F (18°–21°C) to
obtain uniform drainage of the curd. Neither cold and damp nor hot, dry
rooms are suitable. The temperature can be regulated by window ventilation
and by the provision of some sort of heater.

There should be a sufficient area of level shelving and tables or work-
benches. Working surfaces should be of wood which can be well scrubbed,
or else Formica. Hooks can be fixed to the underside of shelves for hanging
the soft cheeses while draining. Plenty of hot water should be available
for the cleaning and sterilization of all equipment used.

In addition, if you are making hard cheese, you will need a suitable
place in which to store the maturing cheese. This should maintain an
even, cool temperature of 50°–60°F (10°–16°C) and should not be too dry
or too damp.

CARE OF EQUIPMENT

It cannot be emphasized too many times that all utensils must be properly
cleaned and sterilized each time they are used. Milk is an ideal medium
for the growth of micro-organisms; inadequate cleaning and sterilization
may lead to its contamination and the consequent spoilage of the cheese.

Immediately after use utensils should be rinsed and scrubbed
thoroughly in cold water. If hot water is used first, a deposit of milk will
be 'baked' onto the surface of the utensil. Next wash and scrub in hot
soapy water. An ordinary kitchen liquid detergent or alternatively
washing soda crystals can be used. Rinse thoroughly in clean hot water
and complete by sterilization.

Sterilization

This can be achieved by: 1. boiling in water;

2. steaming;

3. use of a hypochlorite sterilizing solution.

A large saucepan with a fitted lid can be used for boiling or steaming.
A galvanized clothes boiler is also suitable, but this can only be used on a
gas stove because of its raised bottom. Either immerse the equipment
completely in boiling water, or else place it in a pan with about 2 inches
of boiling water, replace the lid and steam for five minutes. Wooden
boards, cloths and straw mats require special care for they can easily
harbour contaminating organisms. Immerse them in boiling water for at
least 20 minutes. Remember that you cannot boil or steam plastic or
polythene equipment.

Hypochlorite sterilizing solution can be used for much of the equipment
and has the advantage that you are not enveloped in clouds of steam.
Metal utensils other than stainless steel should not be put in the solution
as they will corrode, but it is quite safe for cheese cloths and boards.
Cheese cloths which have been stained by the cheese will regain their
white colour.

If you live on a farm you may have dairy sterilizer available – use it
according to the makers' instructions. Otherwise you can use ordinary
household bleach. This is a solution of sodium hypochlorite and contains
between 4 and 8 per cent (ie. between 40,000 and 80,000 parts per million
[p.p.m.]) of available chlorine. The solution needed for sterilization should
contain between 250 and 500 p.p.m. of available chlorine. The right
concentration can therefore be obtained by diluting 1 fl. oz (2 tablespoons)
of bleach in 1 gallon of water.

Make up your solution in a plastic bucket into which the utensils
can then be placed. Always rinse the utensils thoroughly afterwards with
clean cold water to remove any traces of the hypochlorite which might
otherwise interfere with the cheesemaking bacteria. Leave the utensils
to drain dry, and store them carefully in a clean place. Immediately before
use all equipment should be resterilized.

A dilute solution of hypochlorite can also be used for wiping down
work surfaces and walls in the cheesemaking room.

Ingredients 3

MILK

The milk used for cheesemaking should be of the highest hygienic quality. If you live on a dairy farm or keep a housecow or goat you will have a ready supply of raw milk available. To make sure that this milk is safe and free from contamination or disease-causing organisms, it is advisable to pasteurize it before use (see below).

If you do not have your own supply of milk, and cannot obtain milk direct from a farm, the milk delivered by your local milkman is perfectly suitable. Use pasteurized milk – not sterilized or ultra-heat-treated milk – for cheeses made with rennet; the temperatures used in sterilization and the ultra-heat treatment are higher than the pasteurization temperature and so cause changes in the milk which affect rennet action. (This is explained in the section on the principles of cheesemaking, page 10.)

Pasteurization of the milk

Pour the milk into a stainless steel bucket (do not use a plastic bucket for this) and then place the bucket in a larger container filled with boiling water (illustration 6). Raise the temperature of the milk to 160°F (71°C) for 15 seconds, stirring occasionally to ensure even heating. This is the pasteurization temperature which will kill all the disease-causing organisms.

Bucket of milk

Basin of boiling water

6. Pasteurizing the milk

Cool at once to 40°F (4.5°C) by putting the bucket into cold running water
and keep the milk at this temperature until used; remember that most
bacteria like warm conditions for growth. The milk should be stirred
carefully to prevent a skin forming while cooling, and then covered.
You may find it quicker and easier to pasteurize smaller quantities at a
time.

CREAM

Again if you live on a farm you will have a ready supply of cream available. The section on cream (pages 71–3) gives details of how to separate and pasteurize this cream. If you buy your cream from a dairy or grocer use pasteurized single or double cream depending upon the type of cream cheese you wish to make.

RENNET

Cheese rennet can be obtained in small quantities from a number of suppliers, some of which are listed in the appendix, pp. 84–5. Once obtained the rennet should be kept in a cool dark place, with the stopper tightly secured. Rennet is always measured out immediately before use. Junket rennet, which can be bought at most chemists and grocers, is much weaker than cheese rennet, but can be used as an alternative in some of the soft cheese recipes. Cheese rennet is available in liquid form but junket rennet is now available as tablets. A tablet is ground into a powder and dissolved in cold water first according to the instructions on the packet.

   Rennet activity deteriorates with time even if it is kept in the refrigerator. Before cheesemaking it is advisable to carry out a simple test to check whether the cheese rennet is still suitable for use. Add one drop of rennet from a medical or eye dropper to a dessertspoon of milk previously warmed to between 86° and 98°F (30°–37°C). The milk should set within 5 minutes.

ANNATTO

Annatto is a natural vegetable colouring which can be used if required to give a reddish colour to the cheese.

SALT

The addition of salt helps to preserve the cheese and also to bring out the flavour. Ordinary household salt can be used.

LARD

You will need a good quality lard to coat semi-hard cheeses.

CHEESE STARTER

Cheese starter is milk which contains a special bacterial culture; this is responsible for producing acid during the cheesemaking process and also contributes to the flavour of the cheese. The bacteria in cheese starter use the milk sugar, lactose, for growth, and change it into lactic acid. Most starters used in cheesemaking are controlled cultures of *Streptococcus lactis, Streptococcus cremoris* and *Streptococcus diacetylactis*. These lactic streptococci produce lactic acid very rapidly.

Many of the cheeses in this book require cheese starter. If you live near a cheese creamery or an agricultural college where cheese is made, you may be able to obtain small quantities of starter on the day you wish to make your cheese. Otherwise you will have to obtain an initial supply by post, and then maintain and recultivate it yourself. This requires great care because starter can be easily contaminated.

Recultivation of starter

A newly bought starter will keep for up to three days in a refrigerator. If kept for longer it will deteriorate; the lactic streptococci stored in acid conditions even in the cold lose their viability. Starter can, however, be kept viable by recultivation. This involves the addition of a small amount of starter to fresh sterilized milk to form a new culture which will then grow strongly when kept in warm conditions. Recultivation should be carried out at frequent intervals to ensure that you always have a good, viable starter available. Ideally it should be done every day, but this may prove tedious and time-consuming to the amateur cheesemaker who only makes cheese once a week. So below a way is outlined in which starter can be recultivated just once a week.

Heat treatment of starter bottles and milk   First the bottles and milk used for recultivation must be heat treated. The best way to do this is to heat treat both at the same time, by heating the milk in the bottles. Use screw-cap glass bottles with a narrow neck. They should have a capacity

7. *Suitable bottles for cheese starter cultivation*

of about 6 fl. oz, and should be heat resistant. Sauce bottles or children's orange juice bottles are very suitable (illustration 7). Before using them for the first time wash the bottles very carefully and then immerse them in boiling water for 20 minutes; this will sterilize the bottles and at the same time serve as a test that they can withstand the heat.

You can make up two bottles of culture at a time; one can be used for cheesemaking and the other for recultivation. Pour 5 fl. oz of milk into each bottle and screw the caps on loosely. This is to allow the hot air to escape as the bottles heat up, and to re-enter as the bottles cool; if you screw the caps on too tight, watch out for exploding bottles! Place the bottles in a saucepan with 1–2 inches of water in the bottom. If you have or can make a suitable bottle rack this will prevent the bottles from moving around. Otherwise you can improvise by wedging the bottles with jam jars half full of water, or with other suitable objects (illustration 8).

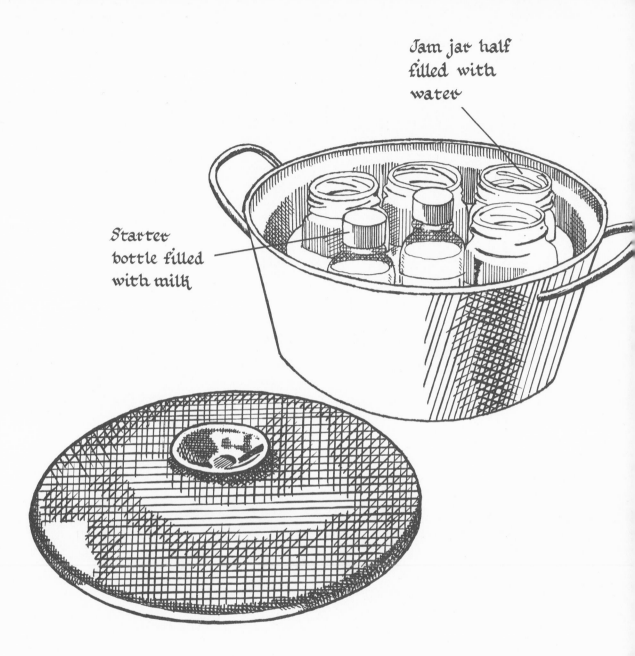

Jam jar half
filled with
water

Starter
bottle filled
with milk

8. *Sterilizing the milk and bottles for the starter*

31

Place the lid on the pan and heat. For adequate sterilization the water should boil continuously for 30 minutes. Remove the bottles and cool until just lukewarm to the touch; do not plunge the hot bottles straight into cold water!

A pressure cooker can also be used. Cover the bottom plate with at least 1 inch of water. Hold the bottles at 15 lbs pressure for 10 minutes. Leave to depressurize for at least 10 minutes. Then cool the bottles.

Transfer of starter   You are now ready to transfer the starter to the new bottles. To help prevent contamination this should be done in an upward current of air, for example in the steam over a saucepan of boiling water (illustration 9) – but take care not to scald yourself. Add ½ teaspoon of starter culture to each bottle of milk, and screw the caps down fully. Shake well. Throw away the remaining contents of the old bottle of starter.

If proper care is taken, the above method of starter transfer works very well for those with limited facilities. However the best way to protect your starter against contamination is to use the *Lewis method*. This involves the use of polythene bottles fitted with special rubber seals. The starter is transferred by piercing the rubber seals with a double-ended inoculating needle, and gently squeezing the bottles. The starter bottles remain airtight throughout the process, and as a result there is little chance of any contamination. The equipment needed, with full instructions for use, can be bought (see appendix for the supplier), but it is relatively expensive and the procedure a little more complicated for the small home cheesemaker. However you may consider it worth the investment.

If, having transferred the starter, you only wish to recultivate it once a week, do not incubate it at once but place the bottle/s in the refrigerator; the starter will keep there for up to a week without deteriorating. The number of bacteria present at this stage is small, and will not produce enough acid to kill the culture.

If you wish to make cheese the next day you can incubate the culture for this immediately.

Incubation of starter   When needed, the starter culture should be incubated in a warm place for 12 hours or until the milk coagulates. Ideally cheese starter should be incubated at 72°F (22°C), but a temperature between 70° and 80°F (21°–27°C) is satisfactory.

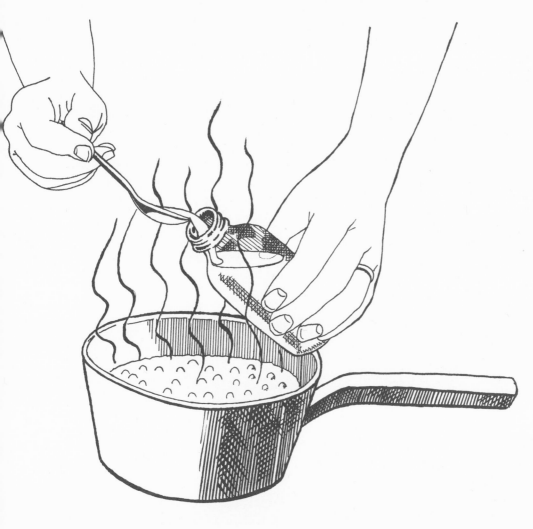

9. *Transferring the starter into the culture bottles*

Incubators

1. *The linen cupboard* – a linen cupboard which maintains a steady temperature is very suitable; check this with a room thermometer. Its disadvantage is that you may not wish to mix your linen with your cheese!

2. *A baby's bottle warmer* – this usually has a selection of temperature settings; you can find the right one by placing a bottle containing water

and a thermometer in the warmer and reading the temperature the water finally reaches at each setting. (I find, with my bottle warmer, that the right temperature is reached when the warmer is just switched on – below setting no. 1.) Only one bottle can be incubated at a time.

3. *An improvised wooden box incubator* – a small wooden box with a light bulb can be rigged up as an incubator, as shown in illustration 10. The size of the box is not important, but the wattage of the light bulb used for heating should be increased or decreased accordingly. To find the right bulb for your box, experiment with different bulbs until the correct temperature is maintained – check this with a thermometer inside the box. (For example, my incubator consists of a modified orange box with a 15-watt bulb.)

The box can be refined further by the addition of inner walls of

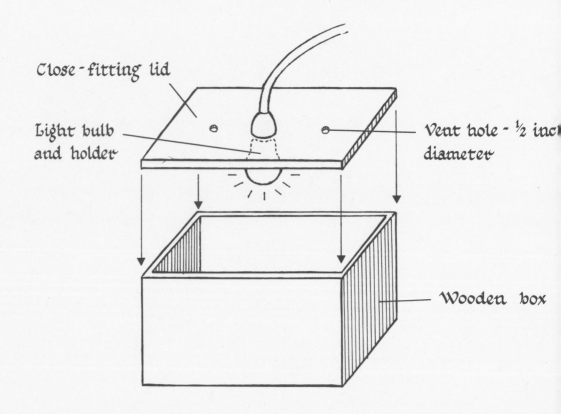

Close-fitting lid

Light bulb and holder

Vent hole - ½ inch diameter

Wooden box

10. An improvised incubator

Formica which can be easily cleaned; and in between these and the outer wooden walls a layer of insulating material such as cotton wool can be inserted to prevent changes in temperature.

This box incubator can also be used to sour milk and cream to make lactic and cream cheese, to ripen cream for butter-making, and to incubate cultured buttermilk and yoghurt culture. Yoghurt culture requires a higher temperature – 110°F (43°C) – and so a more powerful light bulb should be fitted for this. If you wish to incubate larger quantities you can use a larger wooden box.

When the milk in the culture bottle has coagulated, place the culture in a refrigerator until needed for cheesemaking or recultivation later that day. On shaking the coagulated milk, the culture should have a fairly thick but still runny, smooth consistency – similar to a runny yoghurt. After use the bottles should be well washed and sterilized; a bottle brush will help to clean them thoroughly.

If the procedure for starter cultivation seems unduly complicated, the programme suggested overleaf may help to make it clearer.

Note. You may find that over a time the culture becomes weakened and will not set the milk firmly when incubated. If so, throw this away and buy a new culture. It is most important to have a good starter. Remember that a viable starter should give a firm set within 12 hours of the milk being incubated.

An alternative method of starter cultivation using the deep freeze   If you have a deep freeze you can make up a larger number of culture bottles at one time from your initial culture, and then store them in the freezer for up to three months. The bottles of culture can be taken out and used as and when required. This prevents contamination as a result of continuous recultivation, and also saves the time and effort needed each week to recultivate the starter.

Use 4 oz polythene bottles, not glass ones; sterilize the milk and bottles, and transfer the starter as described on page 33. Add just under ½ teaspoon of starter culture to the 4 oz of milk in each bottle and place in the freezer within 20 minutes. When you take a bottle out of the freezer, place it first in hot water at 85°F (29°C) for 2 hours; this helps to bring it up to the right temperature. Then incubate at 70°–80°F (21°–27°C) for 12 hours as before.

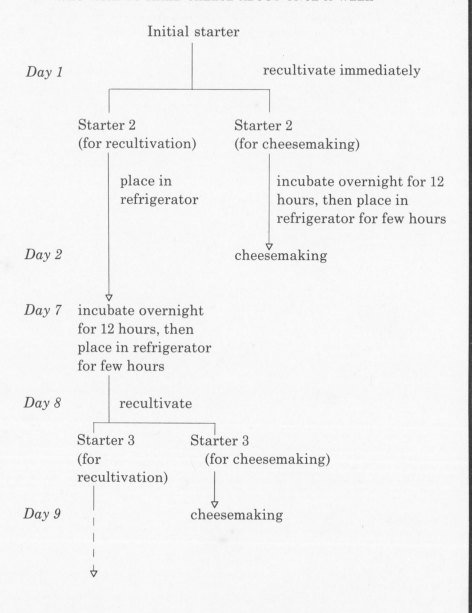

A SUGGESTED PROGRAMME FOR STARTER CULTIVATION FOR THOSE
WHO WISH TO MAKE CHEESE ABOUT ONCE A WEEK

Initial starter

Day 1   recultivate immediately

Starter 2   Starter 2
(for recultivation)   (for cheesemaking)

place in   incubate overnight for 12
refrigerator   hours, then place in
                             refrigerator for few hours

Day 2   cheesemaking

Day 7 incubate overnight
         for 12 hours, then
         place in refrigerator
         for few hours

Day 8   recultivate

Starter 3   Starter 3
(for   (for cheesemaking)
recultivation)

Day 9   cheesemaking

Supply of cheese starter

As mentioned earlier you can obtain cheese starter by post, either in liquid form or as a freeze-dried culture. The latter has the advantage that it will keep practically indefinitely until opened, but then it must be used at once. The freeze-dried culture is reactivated when added to sterilized milk and incubated; it can be recultivated in the same way as the liquid culture.

The instructions with the freeze-dried culture may suggest the use of 1–2 pints of milk for the first cultivation, but these have been written for the commercial cheesemaker who needs a large quantity. You can instead use two bottles each containing 5 fl. oz as before, and add half the contents of your bottle of freeze-dried culture to each one. If you intend to use the deep freeze, recultivate the freeze-dried culture in the ordinary way twice to make sure that the culture is working well, before making up the larger number of bottles for the deep freeze.

A warning to those with a supply of milk direct from a dairy farm

Starter activity can be inhibited by the presence of antibiotics in the milk. Antibiotics are used in the treatment of mastitis and may be present in the milk for some days after treatment has ceased. The milk from treated cows should therefore not be used for cheesemaking for about 2–3 days until the excretion of antibiotics has stopped. This, however, does not apply to those who buy milk from a dairy, since this milk has been bulked from many different farms and it is rare for it to contain inhibitory quantities of antibiotics.

Making Soft Cheeses

4

Note. The recipes in this book have been developed with cow's milk, but goat's milk can also be used. The fat globules in goat's milk are smaller, however, and this influences the temperatures needed for some of the recipes. Renneting temperatures, for example, are lower. Where there is a difference, the relevant temperatures for goat's milk have been indicated.

FRESH MILK CHEESE

If you have never made cheese before, this very simple cheese is a good one to make first and will demonstrate some of the principles involved.

First make a junket with 2 pints of milk. Heat the milk in a double saucepan or in a bowl standing in a saucepan of simmering water, until it reaches 100°F (38°C). Check the temperature with your thermometer. Remove the top saucepan or bowl from the hot water. Dissolve a junket rennet tablet in cold water and add it to the warm milk. Stir well. Cover the bowl and leave in a warm place for two hours until the junket has set.

Next line a colander with a square of muslin. Stand the colander in a bowl (illustration 11). Ladle thin slices of curd into the muslin. You will notice that as you slice into the curd a watery liquid appears; this is the whey. As the whey runs into the bowl underneath and the curd sinks in the colander, add more curd until you have used it all.

Gather the corners of the cloth together and tie a piece of string tightly round it to make a bag. Hang it on a hook with a bowl underneath to catch the whey (illustration 12). Leave it to drain for 1–2 hours.

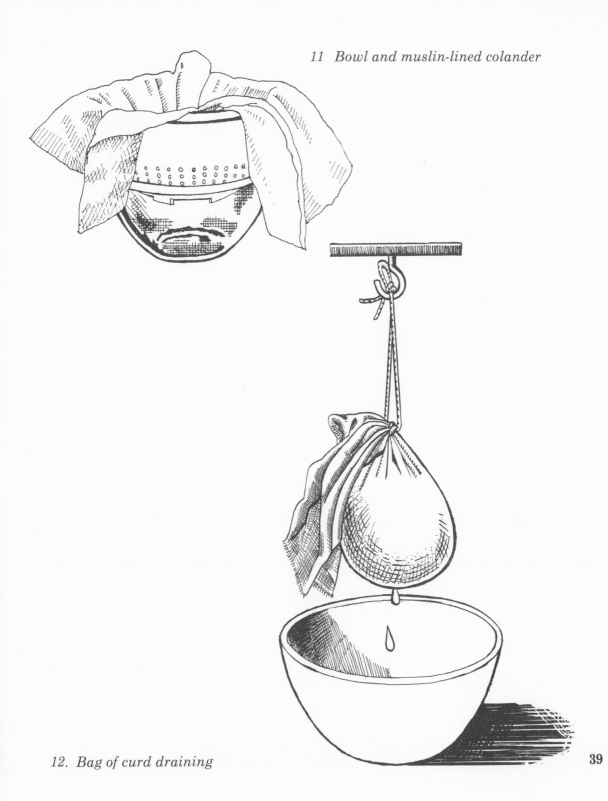

11 *Bowl and muslin-lined colander*

12. *Bag of curd draining*

39

The curd in its bag is now ready to be placed in a soft cheese mould – a Coulommiers hoop or an improvised mould (see page 19). First place the mould on a cheese board, and then place this in a pan to catch the whey (illustration 14 page 45). Put the bag of curd into the mould and leave it for several hours so that the curd takes the shape of the mould. Remember to save the whey. After this the cheese can be carefully removed from the muslin. Wrap it in greaseproof paper and keep it in the refrigerator. It should be eaten within 2–3 days. Two pints of milk will make about 8–10 oz of cheese; it has a bland taste and a smooth texture.

Fresh milk cheese can be eaten in a variety of ways. It is traditionally served swimming in a flat dish of whey, as curds and whey. Pour fresh cream over the top and sprinkle it with caster sugar. Alternatively the solid curd can be eaten with soft or stewed fruit. The whey is a refreshing drink when served cold; it can also be used for mixing scones or cakes. To make a savoury cheese, sprinkle salt on both sides of the curd. You can then press dried herbs such as savory, marjoram or thyme into each side of the curd, or roll it in fine oatmeal.

ACID-CURD CHEESES

These cheeses are formed by the action of acid on the milk protein (see page 15) and are very easy to make. The most simple one of all is a lemon cheese, made with lemon juice. Although it is not a true cheese its manufacture will illustrate the principles involved in making an acid-curd cheese.

Lemon cheese

Heat 1 pint of milk to 100°F (38°C) in a double saucepan or a bowl standing in a saucepan of simmering water. Remove the bowl from the hot water. Add the juice of one lemon to the milk and stir well. Leave for 15 minutes. You will notice that the milk immediately separates into rather stringy curds and whey.

Line a colander with muslin as for the fresh milk cheese (page 38). Ladle the curd into the muslin with a perforated ladle or spoon. Then gather the corners of the cloth together and tie with a piece of string. Hang the bag over a bowl and leave for one hour to drain. Remove the cheese from the muslin; you may have to scrape it off the sides with a knife. Add salt to taste – about $\frac{1}{4}$ teaspoon.

The cheese is now ready to eat. One pint of milk makes 4–5 oz of cheese. It has a moist, spreadable texture and a very pleasant, slightly lemon taste. The whey can be used in baking or served as a cold drink.

Cultured buttermilk cheese

Cultured buttermilk contains a bacterial culture similar to that in a cheese starter. For this cheese you can either buy a pint of fresh cultured buttermilk from your local dairy or grocer, or else make your own as described in the section on buttermilk page 76. The culture in the buttermilk means that it has already coagulated into a thick consistency.

Pour the buttermilk into a double saucepan or bowl and heat slowly over water to 160°F (71°C), stirring occasionally. The heat will cause the curd to separate. Remove the bowl from the hot water, cover it and leave it for about two hours to allow the curd to settle.

Line a colander with muslin as before and tip the contents of the bowl into the muslin. Tie the muslin bag, hang it over a bowl and leave it to drain for two hours. Remove the cheese from the muslin, scraping it off the sides if necessary, and add salt to taste. One pint of buttermilk will make 4–5 oz of cheese; it has a granular, spreadable texture, and a slightly acid taste.

If you want a very moist cheese, only heat the buttermilk to 100°F (38°C). A shorter draining time also gives a moister cheese, and you can experiment to obtain a result to suit your personal taste.

Yoghurt cheese

Yoghurt makes a similar soft cheese. Use fresh natural yoghurt; to buy a pint of yoghurt is relatively expensive, so it is more economical to make your own as described on pages 70–71.

Heat the yoghurt in a double saucepan to 100°F (38°C) and then pour it into the muslin. Hang up the muslin bag and leave it to drain for several hours. Remove the cheese from the muslin and add salt to taste.

This is a moist cheese with a slight acid, yoghurt flavour.

Lactic cheese

In the past this cheese was often made from raw milk which had soured. Now most milk sold is pasteurized, and even if you have your own supply of milk direct from the cow it is still advisable to pasteurize it. Remember it is not safe to use pasteurized milk which has done off for cheesemaking (see page 15), and cheese starter should be used to sour the milk. You can use whole or skimmed milk.

Heat the milk to 75°F (24°C) and add ½ fl. oz (1 tablespoon) of starter to one pint of milk. A better set is obtained if you boil the milk first for one minute and then cool it to 75°F, before adding the starter. You will have to boil the milk directly in a saucepan since it is difficult to raise it to boiling point in a bowl over water. Cover the bowl and leave it in a warm place (70°–80°F, 21°–27°C) for 12 hours or until the milk has coagulated. A linen cupboard or a wooden box incubator are suitable places (see the section on starter cultivation, pages 33–4).

Pour the coagulated milk into a muslin and leave it to drain as before. Add salt to taste. If you are using larger quantities of milk you will find that drainage will take longer – up to two or three days. Drainage can be hastened by opening the cloth at intervals, scraping down the curd on the outside of the cloth and mixing it well with the softer curd in the middle. The cloth can also be changed at intervals.

Packaging

These cheeses are of a fairly runny consistency and you will find it easier to pack them in firm containers. Small polythene containers with lids are excellent, or otherwise you can save old yoghurt and cream cartons. Wash them well and dip them in hypochlorite solution before use to sterilize them. Rinse well. When the cheeses have been packed they can be covered with tinfoil. Keep the cheeses in a cool place or refrigerator, and eat within two to three days.

TRUE SOFT CHEESES

True soft cheeses are made with rennet, although their clean acid flavour is also due to the addition of a bacterial starter culture. Most are made in traditional moulds of a particular shape and size.

Crowdie (or cottage cheese) (similar to American Bakers' cheese)

Crowdie is the old-fashioned Scottish cottage cheese. It is traditionally made from skimmed or separated milk, but you can use whole fat milk.

Heat 2 pints of milk to 90°F (32°C); for goat's milk use 85°F (29°C).

Add 1 fl. oz or 2 tablespoons of cheese starter and one junket rennet tablet dissolved in water (alternatively you can dilute ¼ teaspoon of cheese rennet in six times its own volume of cool, boiled water). Stir well. Cover the bowl and leave in a warm place for about two hours.

When the curd has set, cut it into one inch cubes with a long knife; cut it vertically and then turn the curd over carefully with a spoon and cut it the other way. Now heat the curd to 90°F (32°C), stirring it all the time, and leave it to settle for 10 minutes. Ladle the curd into a muslin and hang it up to drain for several hours.

Remove the cheese from the muslin and add salt. If a slightly richer cheese is required some single cream can be added and mixed thoroughly with the curd. It can then be patted into a rectangular shape and pressed lightly with a cheese board. Wrap it in greaseproof paper, store in the refrigerator and eat within 2 to 3 days.

Coulommiers cheese

The traditional moulds used for Coulommiers cheese are made in two parts, with one hoop fitting into the other (illustration 13). They are so designed that the top section can be removed when the curd has sunk to the level of the bottom one. The moulds are 4–5 inches in diameter and 5–6 inches

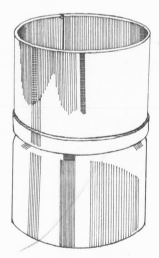

13. Coulommiers moulds

43

high when fitted together. If you do not have the proper moulds then coffee or cocoa tins can be used, as explained on page 19. Choose tins which are about the same size as the complete Coulommiers mould, and cut out their base. One gallon of milk will make three cheeses about 4 inches in diameter and 1½ inches high. If you use 4 pints of milk you can make two slightly smaller cheeses, but remember that all the other ingredients will have to be adjusted in proportion.

Renneting   Heat the milk to 90°F (32°C); for goat's milk use 85°F (29°C). The best way to do this is to place the bucket or bowl of milk in a sink of hot water and stir the milk until the correct temperature is reached. Remove the bucket from the hot water, and add ½ teaspoon of cheese starter to each gallon of milk, stirring well. Then measure out 1 teaspoon of cheese rennet to each gallon of milk, and dilute this with six times its own volume of cool, boiled water to ensure thorough mixing (ie. 1 teaspoon of rennet and 6 teaspoons of water). Add the diluted rennet to the milk and stir in well. Then 'topstir' for about 10 minutes until the milk coagulates. This involves stirring the top ¼ inch of the milk very smoothly and firmly to prevent the fat from rising to the surface. You can tell when coagulation is beginning because the curd will tend to cling to your stirrer as you take it out of the milk. Cover the container and leave for 1–1½ hours or until the curd is firm. To test this push a finger into the curd and out again – if the curd is ready it will split cleanly with a firm edge.

Preparing the moulds   Meanwhile sterilize the moulds, straw mats and cheese boards by boiling them or by using a hypochlorite solution (page 25). Place the moulds on a straw mat and board and stand all this in a shallow pan (illustration 14). If you cannot obtain suitable straw mats, you can use a folded cheese cloth, but make sure that it overhangs the edge of the cheese board slightly to facilitate drainage.

Filling the moulds   First skim off 'tops', which are used later to give a level surface to the cheese: press a mould down on top of the curd, then very carefully scoop out this piece of curd and slide it onto a clean plate or saucer. Cut one top for each mould. Next carefully ladle thin slices of curd and place them evenly in the moulds, lowering the ladle right to the bottom of the mould and letting the curd slip gently into place (illustration 15). It is best to fill all the moulds at the same time so that the curd is

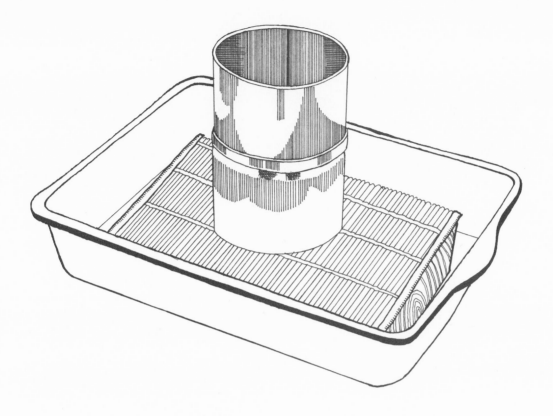

14. The mould standing on a mat and cheese board in a shallow pan

evenly distributed between them and you will finish with cheeses of the same size. Try to avoid breaking the curd, as this will result in a loss of fat and a tough, dry cheese.

The curd's rate of drainage is influenced by the thickness of the layers – thin slices will increase it and thick ones decrease it. If the slices of curd are too thick the whey will drain too slowly. The temperature is important too – if too much heat is lost, the whey will not drain quickly enough and the curd will not sink in the mould. Try to maintain as even a temperature as possible in your cheesemaking room: 60°–70°F (18°–21°C) is ideal.

Go on filling the moulds until the curd reaches the top, then leave for a few minutes until it sinks down a little in the moulds; ladle in more curd until you have used it all. Now slide on the 'tops'. Be careful not to knock the moulds or you will find that the curd shoots out!

45

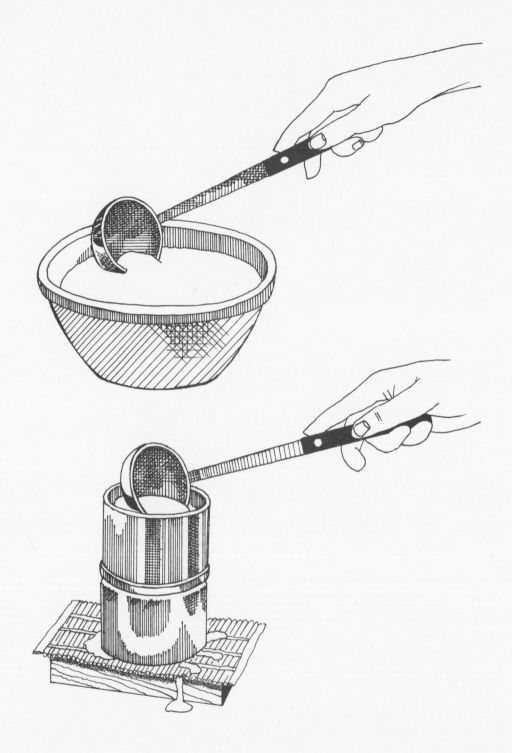

15 Ladling the curd into the mould

Draining and turning   Leave the moulds to drain in a warm place until the curd has sunk below the level of the top hoop (about 24 hours). The top hoop can then be removed and the cheese turned onto a new, freshly sterilized mat and board. The best way to do this is to place the new mat and board on top of the moulds and, holding both boards between your hands, turn them quickly over. Then take away the old board and carefully remove the mat, so that the cheese comes away free and does not stick to it (illustration 16, overleaf).

If you do not have the double moulds and so cannot remove a top section, take great care with the turning as the cheese will fall some distance from the top to the bottom of the mould and can easily be damaged or spoilt. Remember to clean and sterilize the old mat and board immediately after use.

Continue to turn the cheeses onto fresh mats and boards every 24 hours until they are firm. By the third day the curd should have drained enough to leave the sides of the moulds. Remove the moulds and rub about ½ oz of salt into the surface of each cheese.

If the cheeses require further firming they can be drained out of the mould and turned every day, but at this stage must be kept in a cool, dry atmosphere. The surface of the cheese may become mouldy; if so wipe off any mould with a damp cloth dipped in cold water and put the cheese in a colder, drier place.

The cheese can be eaten immediately but will be found to improve if kept in a refrigerator or cool place for a couple of days. Lightly wrap in greaseproof paper and eat within a week.

Colwick cheese

Colwick is an English soft cheese and was traditionally made in a single perforated cylindrical mould about 7 inches high and 5 inches in diameter. However the moulds are no longer available and Coulommiers moulds can be used instead. The top hoop will not be removed since the cheese is not turned. If improvised moulds are used, the base of the tin should be cut away and holes pierced in the sides. One gallon of milk will make two cheeses; 4 pints will make one cheese.

Renneting   Heat the milk to 90°F (32°C) for cow's milk, 85°F (29°C) for goat's milk. Add ½ teaspoon of cheese starter and 1 small teaspoon of cheese rennet (diluted with six times its own volume of water) to each

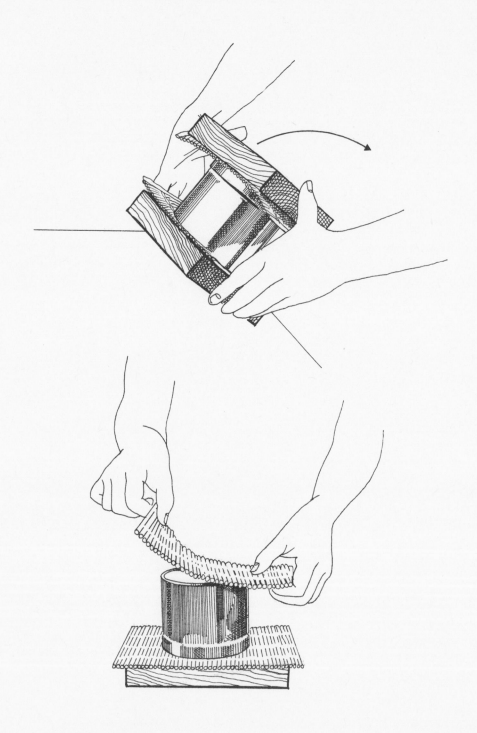

16 Turning the mould onto a new mat and board

gallon of milk; stir in well. Topstir for about 10 minutes until coagulation begins, then cover the container and leave for 1–1½ hours until the curd is firm.

Preparing the moulds   Set up the moulds on the straw mat and cheese board in a shallow pan as before (page 44), but this time line each mould with a cheese cloth large enough to fold over the top of the curd.

Filling the moulds and draining   Slice off two 'tops' and place them in clean saucers. Ladle the curd in thin slices into the moulds as before, leave to drain a little and slide on the tops. Leave to drain for an hour, then pull the muslin upwards and inwards so that the curd is pulled away from the sides of the mould. This produces the characteristic curling over of the edge of Colwick cheese. Repeat at intervals during the next four hours. The cheese is not turned; allow it to drain for 24–36 hours when it should be firm enough to handle. Remove the mould and pull the muslin very carefully away from the cheese.

The cheese is now ready to eat, but should be stored in a refrigerator if not eaten immediately. It can be salted, but traditionally it is not, and is served either as a sweet or a savoury. The hollow in the centre can be filled with whipped cream.

Cambridge or York cheese

This is another English soft cheese which used to be made around the Isle of Ely and was sold in the markets of Cambridge. The traditional moulds were rectangular and made in two parts; the top portion was about 7–8 inches long, 4–5 inches wide and 6 inches deep, and was placed in a shallow tray holding a fitted piece of straw mat. The cheese was served on its straw mat. These moulds are no longer available, but you can improvise with square or rectangular cake tins from which the base has been cut. The square tins 6 × 6 inches are very suitable, and can be placed straight onto the straw mat or cheese cloth without the traditional tray.

1½ gallons of milk will make two cheeses weighing ¾–1 lb each; 6 pints will make one cheese. Cambridge cheese is not salted and has a coloured stripe running through the middle.

Renneting   Heat the milk to 90°F (32°C); for goat's milk use 85°F (29°C). To each 1½ gallons of milk add 1 teaspoon of starter and 1 teaspoon of cheese rennet diluted in water. Stir in well for a minute or two and then if you want a coloured stripe in the middle of your cheese remove 4 pints from each 1½ gallons of milk and place in another container. To this add 1 teaspoon of annatto and stir in until the colour is uniform. Do not topstir the remaining milk, as this cheese has a creamy top. Cover both containers and leave for 1–1½ hours until firm and the curd splits cleanly over the finger.

Filling the moulds and draining   Sterilize the moulds, a straw mat or cheese cloth and a board and set up as before (illustration 14, page 45). Slice off the creamy tops by pressing a mould on top of the uncoloured curd where the cream has risen and skimming carefully off. Place the tops on clean plates. Then ladle thin layers of curd into the moulds; first ladle out about two-thirds of the plain, uncoloured curd, then all the coloured curd, and finish off with the remaining uncoloured curd before positioning the tops. You will find that when drainage is complete the coloured stripe will be roughly in the centre of the cheese.

Leave the curd to drain in the moulds for 2–3 days. Do not turn or add any salt. When the cheese is firm enough the moulds can be removed and the cheeses carefully lifted from the mat. They are now ready to eat and should be stored in a cool place. If mould begins to develop on the cheese surface, it should be wiped off; further mould growth can be prevented by leaving a clean piece of blotting paper on the surface to soak up the whey until the cheese is eaten.

Traditionally this cheese is cut into three portions for serving. It has a sharp, cleanly acid flavour.

CREAM CHEESES

Cream cheeses are traditionally moulded into small cylindrical, square or rectangular shapes of various sizes and weights. Unfortunately the small metal moulds are no longer available, but you can improvise in various ways.

Single cream cheese

This is made from single cream as its name suggests, and needs rennet for coagulation. Single cream has a butterfat content of 18–25 per cent.

Heat 1 pint of single cream to 75°F (24°C). Add ½ teaspoon of cheese starter and mix well. Cover the bowl and leave in a warm place for 2–3 hours to allow the cream to ripen. Alternatively you can use freshly bought soured cream. But do not use pasteurized cream which has gone sour! Warm the soured cream to 75°F.

Next dilute ¼ teaspoon of rennet with six times its own volume of cold boiled water, and add this to the cream, stirring well to mix. Cover the bowl and leave in a warm place or incubator at 70°–80°F (21°–27°C) for 8–12 hours or until the cream coagulates (see the section on starter cultivation, pages 33–5).

Ladle the coagulum in slices into a thick cloth (2 cheese cloths put together work very well). Hang it up to drain in a cool, well-ventilated room – 50°–55°F (10°–13°C). Alternatively the bag of curd can be placed horizontally between two cheese boards with a 1–2 lb weight on top. The boards can then be placed in a tin to collect the whey. This hastens the draining process.

During the draining period the cloth should be opened at 4–8 hourly intervals and the curd on the outside near the cloth scraped down and mixed well with the softer curd in the middle. The more often this is done the quicker the curd will drain. If the cloth becomes clogged with curd drainage will be restricted. The cloth should be changed at intervals. When sufficiently drained the curd will have a thick, rather granular consistency. Add salt and mix well.

The cheese can be shaped into a round pat and wrapped in grease-proof paper or tinfoil, or packed into plastic cartons. Keep it in the refrigerator and eat within 2–3 days.

Double cream cheese

Double cream drains without rennet, but the addition of starter results in quicker drainage and a pleasant, slightly acid flavour to the cheese. It also improves its keeping quality. Double cream has a butterfat content of 48–55 per cent.

Heat 1 pint of double cream to 75°F (24°C); add ½ teaspoon of starter and ¼ oz of salt and stir well. Salting the cream at this stage helps it to drain well and improves its keeping quality. Cover the cream and leave it in a warm place to coagulate as before. Ladle it into a thick cloth and hang it up to drain in a cool place. Then treat as for single cream cheese.

WHEY CHEESES

When making cheese you will find that you have large quantities of whey left over. Do collect this – it can be used in baking or served as a cool refreshing drink. You can also try making whey cheeses.

Whey cheese

You will need 1 pint of whey to 2 pints of fresh milk. Pour the whey directly into a saucepan and heat very slowly until bubbles begin to appear, then pour in the fresh milk. Continue heating for about ten minutes, stirring occasionally. Do not let the liquid boil. You will notice that the curd begins to separate. Take it off the heat, and cover the pan. Leave it for two hours to allow the curd to settle, then pour it into muslin. Hang up the muslin bag and drain for 2–3 hours. Add salt to taste, then pack it into plastic or polythene containers. Keep the cheese in a refrigerator and eat within 2–3 days.

Mysost cheese

Pour the whey into a saucepan and heat very slowly until the whey has evaporated to a thick treacle. This will take several hours. Then cool it rapidly by standing the pan in cold water. When cool the cheese should be the colour of honey, and have the consistency of butter. Pack it in small glass jars and seal tightly. Two pints of whey will make about 4 oz of cheese.

This cheese has a very strong smell and flavour, and you may find it an acquired taste!

Making Semi-Hard Cheeses

5

SEMI-HARD CHEESE

Hard cheeses are not easy to make in the home because of the difficulty of applying enough pressure to press them really hard. However, with improvised moulds and weights, it is possible to make a semi-hard cheese. This requires a little more time and skill than soft cheese, but you will find there is a great sense of achievement in producing your own 'hard' cheese.

The importance of having acidity developing at a steady rate throughout the cheesemaking process has already been discussed in the section on the principles of cheesemaking, pages 10–11. The commercial cheesemaker can measure the acidity at various stages by chemical tests. This is difficult for the small home cheesemaker, but the development of acidity can be judged by physical changes in the curd. These are explained in the recipes and will be learned with experience.

You will need to put aside a whole day (especially the first time) and have no other commitments since the cheese will need your attention for much of the time, and the process should not be hurried.

The quantity of milk involved is somewhat larger than that required for soft cheese so remember to place an order with your milkman. If you live on a dairy farm or have your own cow or goat it is best to mix milk from the morning and evening milkings in equal proportions; evening milk is richer in fat than morning milk, and a mixture of the two milkings

will result in a milk with a better fat content for hard cheesemaking.
A high fat milk gives a soft velvety curd.

All the recipes in this section use 2 gallons of milk because this
amount is convenient to handle in a 2 or 2½ gallon bucket. The 6-inch cake
tin mould (illustration 2, page 20) will just take the curd from 2 gallons of
milk, and 2 gallons will make about 2 lbs of cheese. If you have larger milk
containers and a larger cheese mould and press you can use more milk,
but remember to adjust all the other quantities in proportion.

A Smallholder cheese is a good one to try first. Each stage is
described in detail. Once you have mastered this you can try one of the
other recipes. You will see that the same processes are involved for each
type of cheese; only the times and temperatures are different to give the
variety in flavour and texture. The Caerphilly-type and Small Cheshire
contain more moisture and less acidity than their larger sized namesakes.

Before you start gather together all the equipment necessary and
sterilize it.

SMALLHOLDER CHEESE (American Farm cheese)

Ripening   Pour the milk into a suitable bucket and heat to 90°F (32°C),
or for goat's milk 85°F (29°C). This can be done by placing the bucket in
a sink of hot water and stirring the milk until the correct temperature is
reached. Then take the bucket out of the hot water, otherwise the temperature of the milk will continue to rise. Add 2 fl. oz or 4 tablespoons of
cheese starter and stir in well. Cover the bucket with a cheese cloth and
leave for 45 minutes.

Renneting   Use cheese rennet only. You need 1 teaspoon of rennet for
each 2 gallons of milk. Dilute it with three times its own volume of cold
boiled water; this should be measured immediately before use. Check that
the temperature of the milk is still 90°F (32°C), or for goat's milk 85°F
(29°C), and if necessary bring it back to this temperature by replacing
the bucket in the sink of hot water. Pour the diluted rennet carefully into
the milk, and stir at once right down to the bottom of the bucket for half
a minute. Then topstir (see page 44) until coagulation begins. Ideally this
should take 10–15 minutes. You will be able to tell when coagulation is
near because the curd feels dense and the bubbles stay on the surface
instead of breaking.

54

The time that the rennet takes to coagulate the milk is an indication of the rate of acid development. If the milk sets in 10–15 minutes the acidity is developing at a good, steady rate. If the milk sets in less than 10 minutes then the acidity is developing fast; this may happen because the starter is very vigorous, the milk is dirty or the weather hot. If the milk takes longer than 15 minutes to set, then acidity is developing slowly, perhaps because the starter is not very active. High or low acid development can result in spoilt cheese. However, by adjusting the degree and length of scalding (explained page 12), it is possible to keep pace with the development of acidity, and so save your cheese.

When the milk has coagulated, cover the bucket and leave for about 45 minutes or until the curd is firm enough to split cleanly over your finger – again this time will depend on the rate of acid development. If the milk is left too long the whey will begin to separate out in pools on the surface of the curd.

Cutting the curd   Both this stage and the scalding stage which comes next are a vital part of cheesemaking, and should not be hurried. The cutting and scalding allow the whey to drain from the curd particles. If the drainage happens too quickly the curd will become tough and the cheese will be leathery. Carefully cut the curd into $\frac{1}{4}$–$\frac{1}{2}$ inch cubes. Make the first cuts with an ordinary stainless steel carving knife; holding it vertically, cut down and across the curd in one direction and then down and across it at right angles to the first cuts (illustration 17, top). Then, following the lines of these vertical cuts, cut the curd at an angle, diagonally, first in one direction and then in the other (illustration 17, bottom). Turn the curd over carefully in the bucket and stir it gently for about 5 minutes. Check that all the curd pieces are fairly even and cut up those that are too big.

Scalding   The curd is now ready for scalding. Again stand your bucket in a sink of hot water, and take about 30 minutes to heat the curd slowly and steadily to 100°F (38°C), or for goat's milk 95°F (35°C). Stir gently all the time to prevent the curd pieces from sticking together. It is generally better to heat the curd slowly at first, and then accelerate towards the end. You will notice that the curd pieces shrink in size and become firmer – when you scoop them up in your hand they should be firm enough to separate easily. To ensure that they are properly firm you can keep the curds and whey at 100°F (38°C) for a longer time (still stirring) until they

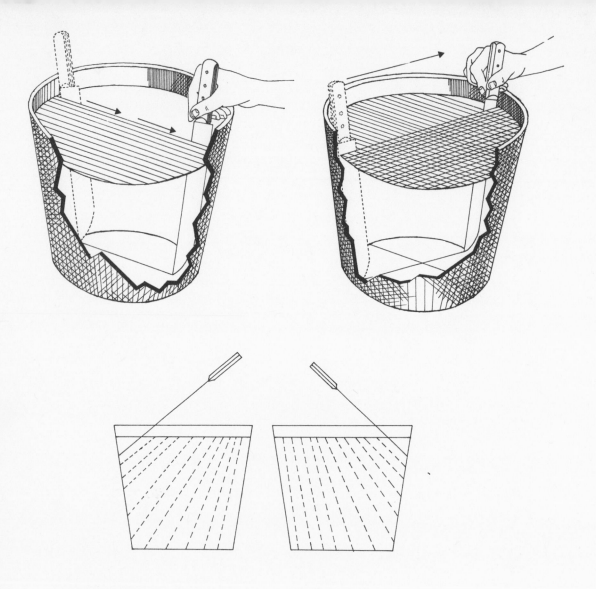

17 *Cutting the curd into cubes*

separate even when squeezed in the hand.

    If there has been an indication during renneting that the acidity is developing fast the curd must be drained of whey more quickly. This is done by scalding it to a higher temperature in a shorter time (eg. 105°F [41°C] in 20 minutes). If the curd is 'working slowly', slow scalding to a lower temperature (eg. 98°F [37°C] in 40 minutes) will result in slower drainage of whey. In either case the curd pieces should become firm and resilient, and separate easily when held or squeezed in the hand.

Draining the whey   Allow the curd to settle for a few minutes before draining. To drain the whey, tie a cloth over a spare bucket and then very gently tip the contents of the first bucket onto the cloth, so that the whey goes into the bucket and the curd remains in the cloth (illustration 18). You may find it easier to do this with two people. Afterwards tie up the corners of the cloth and make a bundle of the curd, put it back in the empty bucket and leave it to consolidate for about an hour, tightening the muslin every ten minutes or so to expel more whey (illustration 19). The curd should now have a rubbery texture and should make a squeaky sound when a small piece is chewed.

18 Pouring off the whey into a spare bucket

19 *The curd wrapped in a bundle*

Salting   Break the curd up cleanly into small pieces the size of a
walnut, taking care not to squeeze out any fat. Turn the pieces over
several times to allow them to cool and drain. Sprinkle on salt – $\frac{2}{3}$ oz to
2 gallons of milk – and mix it in well.

Moulding and pressing the curd   Line your mould (page 19) with a damp
cheese cloth and pack in the curd as evenly as possible. Place smaller
pieces of curd in the mould first, pack in the rest of the curd, and then
finish off with small pieces; this will give a better finish to the top and
bottom of the cheese. Fold the cheese cloth over the curd, and place
the wooden follower on top of this. Put weights up to 28 lbs on top.
Remember to stand the mould in a pan to collect the whey.

After a few hours take the cheese out of the press and turn it. Wrap
it in a dry cloth, and then put it back into the mould under increased
pressure – up to 40 lbs if possible. The next day turn the cheese again,
using a new cloth, and place it back in the mould under as much weight
as possible. Leave for 24 hours.

Finishing the cheese   The simplest way to do this is to melt some lard and coat the surface of the cheese with a very thin layer. For a 2 lb cheese you will need 1–2 oz of lard.

The cheese will keep better if it is bandaged as well. Cut some pieces of butter muslin – two round pieces slightly wider than the cheese for the top and the bottom, and one long piece to go round the cheese. Lay the muslin flat on the top and bottom, smoothing it down well; then wrap the long piece around, pulling the edges together to exclude the air (illustration 20). If you do not bandage the cheese, the outside surface should be rubbed over at intervals with a clean cloth to stop the development of mould.

Maturing the cheese   The cheese can be left to mature for 6–8 weeks before it is ready for eating; it will than have a firm body and a mild flavour. Store it in a cool place, neither too dry nor too damp, and which maintains an even temperature of 50°–60°F (10°–16°C). Place the cheese

20 *Bandaging the cheese*

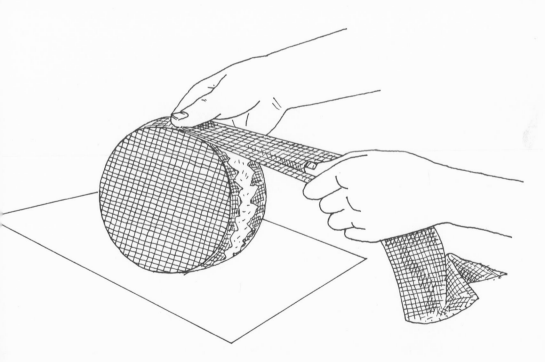

on a shelf so that the air can circulate around it. At first the cheese should be turned every day, then three times a week and later once a week. If any cracks appear cover them with melted lard.

CAERPHILLY-TYPE CHEESE

Ripening   Heat the milk to 90°F (32°C) for cow's milk, 85°F (29.5°C) for goat's milk. Add 6 fl. oz of cheese starter, and then cover and leave to ripen for 30 minutes.

Renneting   Add 1 teaspoon of rennet (diluted with water) to each 2 gallons of milk. Stir thoroughly for ½ minute and then topstir until coagulation begins. Cover and leave for 45 minutes, or until the curd is firm.

Cutting   Cut the curd as before (page 55). Turn it over carefully.

Scalding   Heat as quickly as possible to 92°F (33.5°C), or for goat's milk 87°F (31°C). Keep the curd at this temperature and stir for 40 minutes. If acidity is developing fast make adjustments as before (heat to 95°F [35°C] and keep at this temperature for 30 minutes). To test whether the curd is ready yet press the hand firmly onto it; if it is ready the pattern of your skin will appear on the curd and stay there. If this does not happen after 40 minutes (because for example acidity is developing slowly), go on stirring at the same temperature until it does.

Draining the whey   Let the curd settle in the whey, then pour this off at once. Leave the curd piled to one side of the bucket for 5 minutes and pour off any further whey that has accumulated. Cut the heap of curd into slices vertically and then horizontally (illustration 21, top). Spread these slices on one side of the bucket, leaving a channel for the whey to escape. This is made easier if you tip the bucket slightly (illustration 21, bottom). Turn over all the pieces of curd twice in 10 minutes.

Salting   Break up the curd into walnut-size pieces, and add salt – 1 oz to each 4 lbs of curd.

Moulding and pressing   Line your mould with a damp cheese cloth, pack it with curd, fold over the muslin, and then place the follower and

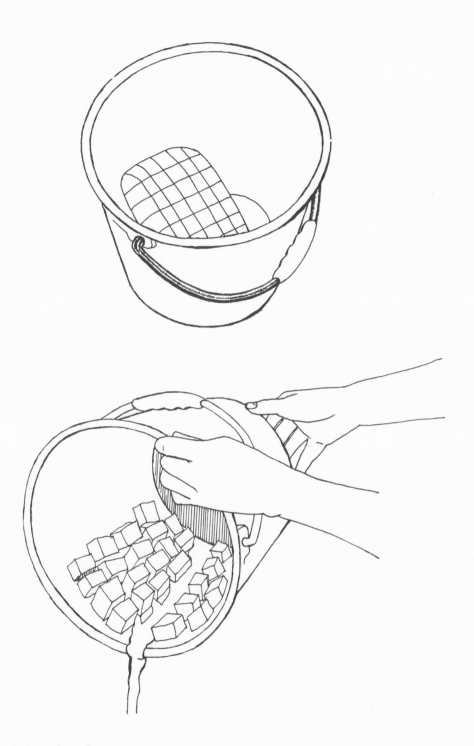

21 *Draining the whey*

4 lbs of weights on top. Take the cheese out after 10 minutes and turn it; repeat twice more at 10-minute intervals, then leave the cheese under the weights for 14–16 hours.

Finishing   Remove the cheese from the mould and dry off the surface with a dry cloth. Lard and bandage as described page 59.

Maturing   Leave the cheese in a cool place for about 14 days to ripen; remember to turn it daily.

SMALL CHESHIRE CHEESE

Ripening   Heat the milk to 85°F (29°C), and add 4 fl. oz of cheese starter. Leave for 45 minutes.

Renneting   Add annatto if required for a red Cheshire colour – ½ teaspoon to 2 gallons of milk. Mix in 1 teaspoon of rennet diluted in water. Stir thoroughly for ½ minute, and then topstir until coagulation takes place. Leave for 45–60 minutes.

Cutting   Cut the curd as before (illustration 17, page 56); turn it over carefully.

Scalding   Raise the temperature of the curd very slowly, taking 1 hour to reach 93°F (34°C) and stirring all the time. If acidity is developing fast you can heat it more quickly. Then go on stirring until the curd particles are firm and separate easily in the hand.

Draining the whey   Let the curd settle for about 15 minutes, then pour off the whey. Leave the curd to mat together for 5 minutes, then cut it into blocks and turn each block over. Do this again twice, then break each block into pieces and turn it again, taking care not to crush the curd. Repeat three times at 10-minute intervals.

Salting   Break the curd into walnut-size pieces. Sprinkle salt over it – 1 oz to 3 lbs of curd – and mix well. Stir the curd to cool it.

Moulding and pressing   Pack the curd into a muslin-lined mould, place a follower and up to 8 lbs of weights on top. Remove the cheese after one hour, turn it and put it back in the mould under the weights. The next day turn the cheese again, wrap it in a new cloth and replace it in the mould. Leave for 24 hours.

Finishing   Lard and bandage as before (page 59).

Maturing   Leave it to ripen for 4–6 weeks in a cool place. Turn regularly.

Cooking with Home-Made Cheeses

6

Cheese is an extremely versatile food and can be used for cooking a variety of dishes. Many of your own favourite cheese recipes can be made with the semi-hard cheeses described in this book. Since you may not be as familiar with recipes using 'soft' cheeses, I have selected a few representative examples to show how it too can be used in cooking. You will be able to collect many more recipes as you progress and experiment.

Use acid-curd cheese or Crowdie for preference; the true soft cheeses such as Coulommiers or Cambridge are best eaten straight, so that their taste, texture, colour and shape can be properly appreciated. Cream cheese can be used in many ways; it is ideal for spreads and dips. Yoghurt too is an important ingredient of many recipes.

Cheesecake Pie (Serves 4)

Shortcrust pastry made with 4 oz flour	1 egg
4 oz acid-curd cheese	1 oz self-raising flour
1 oz butter (softened)	$\frac{1}{8}$ pint milk
2 oz caster sugar	1 teaspoon grated lemon rind

Line a 6-inch flan tin with pastry. Bake 'blind' at mark 6, 400°F (200°C), for 15 minutes. (To bake blind line the pastry with aluminium foil – this prevents the pastry rising as it cooks. Remove the foil before filling the pastry case.) Mix together the cheese, soft butter, caster sugar, beaten egg, flour, milk and lemon rind. Spoon the cheese mixture into the flan case and bake for 20–30 minutes at mark 4, 350°F (180°C), until the filling has set. Turn off the heat, allow the pie to cool slowly in the oven – this will help to prevent it sinking in the middle. Serve hot or cold.

Austrian Curd Cheesecake

2 oz butter or margarine
3 oz caster sugar
2 eggs
½ teaspoon vanilla essence

8 oz acid-curd cheese
2 oz self-raising flour
1 tablespoon milk
1 oz sultanas

Grease an 8-inch square shallow tin and dust with flour. You can line it with greaseproof paper to ensure that the cake turns out easily. Cream the butter and sugar. Beat in the eggs, one at a time, and add the vanilla. Beat in the cheese until the mixture is light and smooth. Stir in the flour, milk and sultanas and spread evenly in the prepared tin. Bake at mark 4, 350°F (180°C), for 40 minutes until the cake is firm and set. Allow the cake to cool in the oven slowly, and then turn out onto a rack. Cut the cake into fingers and dust the top with icing sugar.

Cheese and Pineapple Dip

8 oz acid-curd cheese
4 tablespoons single cream
4 tablespoons finely chopped pineapple

Salt and pepper
Chopped red and green peppers

Mix the cheese with the cream and pineapple. Season to taste. Garnish with red and green peppers. Chill well before serving.

Yoghurt Salad Dressing

5 oz natural yoghurt
2 tablespoons single cream
3 teaspoons lemon juice

1 level teaspoon caster sugar
Salt and pepper

Beat together the yoghurt, cream, lemon juice and sugar. Season to taste with salt and pepper. Chill before using.

Cream Cheese and Fruit Flan (Serves 4)

Shortcrust pastry made with 4 oz flour
4 oz cream cheese
2 oz caster sugar
Fresh soft fruit or tinned fruit
2 tablespoons apricot jam

Line a 6-inch flan tin with pastry. Bake 'blind' at mark 6, 400°F (200°C), until crisp and golden brown. (Line the pastry with aluminium foil, bake for 15 minutes, then remove the foil and return the flan to the oven to bake for a further 15 minutes.) Cream the cheese and sugar together, then spread evenly over the bottom of the flan case. Chill for at least 1 hour. Arrange soft or drained tinned fruit on top of the cheese mixture. Warm the apricot jam with 2 tablespoons of hot water, sieve and then spoon carefully over the fruit as a glaze.

Coeur à la Crême (Serves 4)

8 oz acid-curd cheese
2 oz caster sugar

2 tablespoons double cream
2 egg whites

Sieve the cheese, and mix in the sugar and cream. Whisk the egg whites until stiff, then fold into the cheese mixture. Spoon into 4 individual dishes and chill. Serve with fresh soft fruit and cream.

Slimmers Coeur à la Crême (Serves 4)

8 oz acid-curd cheese
5 oz natural yoghurt

Juice of $\frac{1}{2}$ lemon
2 egg whites

Sieve the cheese and mix with the yoghurt and lemon juice. Whisk the egg whites until stiff, then fold into the cheese mixture. Spoon into 4 individual dishes and chill. Serve with fresh soft fruit.

Savoury Flan (Serves 4)

Shortcrust pastry made with 4 oz flour $\frac{1}{8}$ pint milk
4 oz streaky bacon   4 oz acid-curd cheese
2 eggs   Salt and pepper

Line a 6-inch flan case with pastry. Cut the bacon rashers into small
pieces and fry until cooked. Drain off the fat and arrange the bacon
pieces in the bottom of the flan case. Beat together the eggs, milk, cheese,
salt and pepper, and pour into the flan case. Bake at mark 4, 350°F (180°C),
for 30 minutes or until the filling is set and golden brown. Serve hot or
cold.

Cream Cheese and Yoghurt Dip

5 oz natural yoghurt   1 level teaspoon paprika
4 oz cream cheese   Salt and pepper
2 tablespoons finely chopped peeled cucumber

Beat the yoghurt into the cheese. Stir in the cucumber and paprika.
Season to taste. Chill well before serving.

Cheese Stuffed Tomatoes

4 large tomatoes
4 oz acid-curd or cream cheese
1 stick celery, chopped
1 eating apple, chopped
1 spring onion, chopped, or 1 level tablespoon chopped chives
Salt and pepper

Cut the tops off the tomatoes and scoop out the centres. Mix the centres
with the other ingredients, and add salt and pepper to taste. When ready
to serve divide the mixture between the tomatoes and replace the lids.

Savoury Cream Cheese Flan (Serves 4)

Shortcrust pastry made with 4 oz flour
4 oz cream cheese
Garnishings – sliced cucumber, hard-boiled egg, onion rings,
                radishes or ham rolls

Line a 6-inch flan tin with pastry. Bake 'blind' at mark 6, 400°F (200°C), until crisp and golden brown. Spread the cream cheese evenly over the bottom of the flan case. Decorate with a selection of the garnishings. Serve very cold with a salad.

Chilled Lemon Cheesecake (Serves 4)

Biscuit base: 6 digestive biscuits
                1 oz butter
                1 oz sugar
Filling: $\frac{1}{2}$ lemon jelly
                1 egg – separated
                4 oz acid-curd cheese
                5 oz natural yoghurt
                lemon rind and the juice from $\frac{1}{2}$ lemon

Break the digestive biscuits into crumbs and mix well with the softened butter and sugar. Line a flan ring with the biscuit-crumb mixture, pressing down well. Put it into the refrigerator to harden. Add 2 tablespoons of hot water to the jelly pieces. Continue to melt the jelly in a bowl over hot water. Allow to cool slightly. Beat in the egg yolk, sieved cheese, yoghurt, lemon rind and juice. Fold in the whisked egg white, and pour the mixture into the biscuit crust. Replace in the refrigerator to set.

Other Dairy Products 7

YOGHURT

Yoghurt is a cultured milk. It has only comparatively recently become popular in this country, but different cultured milks have been consumed for centuries in Eastern Europe, and in the countries of the Near, Middle and Far East.

Cultured milk is produced by the action of bacterial micro-organisms which change the lactose (milk sugar) into lactic acid. The result is an acid-curd. In hot countries these soured or cultured milks are considered the best way to consume milk, since the lactic acid acts as a preservative and keeps the milk in a palatable form.

There is a great range of cultured milks; yoghurt, for example, is the traditional cultured milk of the Balkans – Greece, Turkey and Bulgaria. The differences in taste and texture between the various forms of cultured milk depend partly on the type of milk used – it may come from cows, goats, sheep, buffaloes or even mares – and partly on the type of bacterial micro-organism present; each type provides its own characteristic flavour. The flavour and texture of yoghurt is imparted by a culture which consists of equal proportions of *Lactobacillus bulgaricus* and *Streptococcus thermophilus*.

'Live' yoghurt

Some people believe that only yoghurts labelled 'live' or 'true' contain the live yoghurt culture; this is not so. All yoghurts sold in this country are made from a live culture. After incubation the yoghurt is cooled and then kept at a low temperature. This arrests the growth of the culture but does not kill it.

Food value

Various therapeutic benefits have been attributed to yoghurt, but the original theory that yoghurt possesses unique properties which ensure a long and healthy life has not been proved. Nevertheless, because it is made from milk, yoghurt is an excellent food. Most commercially produced yoghurts are made from a skimmed-milk base and have a low fat content. The fruit yoghurts have added fruit and sugar of course, so the milk nutrients are reduced accordingly.

Yoghurt is a food which appeals to and can be eaten by people of all ages. Because it is easily digested it is very suitable for babies (from about 6 months onwards) and for old people.

Making yoghurt at home

There are various yoghurt-making machines on the market and you may wish to invest in one. However these are relatively expensive and other suitable incubators can be improvised.

You will need a saucepan, a tablespoon, a thermometer and a room thermometer, a suitable container for incubating the yoghurt, a fresh carton of yoghurt or yoghurt culture and of course the milk.

First sterilize all the equipment as described on page 25. Raw or pasteurized milk should be boiled for one minute first, then cooled to 110°F (43°C); the milk should be stirred carefully to prevent a skin forming while cooling. Alternatively sterilized or ultra-heat-treated milk can be used for yoghurt (although not for making cheese); these types of milk need not be boiled, but can just be heated to 110°F (43°C).

Now add $\frac{1}{2}$ fl. oz (1 tablespoon) of natural yoghurt to each pint of milk and mix well. Make sure from the date code that the yoghurt you use is as fresh as possible. Yoghurt caps should be secure and not 'blown'. Buy from chilled cabinets only. Alternatively a yoghurt culture can be used – this can be obtained by post (see list in appendix for suppliers).

Pour the milk into a suitable container or containers – you can use old yoghurt cartons (washed and sterilized) for individual yoghurts. Cover and leave in a warm place for 3–4 hours to allow the yoghurt to set. The yoghurt culture needs a temperature of about 110°F (43°C) at which to grow; this is higher than that required for cheese starter. Your linen cupboard may maintain a temperature as high as this – check with a room thermometer – or use a wooden box incubator (as described in the section on starter cultivation page 33–5).

Alternatively a wide-necked vacuum flask can be used as an incubator; it will maintain the temperature of the milk. Pour the milk into the flask and leave this in a warm place for 3–4 hours to allow the yoghurt to set. Remember that it will need careful cleaning and sterilization afterwards. Or you can use a baby's bottle warmer. Find the appropriate setting as described before in the section on starter cultivation page 33. (I find, with my bottle warmer, that a temperature of 110°F [43°C] is reached at setting no. 1.) The bottle warmer however will only hold a baby's bottle or similar sized container, so you will not be able to make more than a small quantity – $\frac{1}{2}$ pint – at a time. Again the yoghurt will take about 3 hours to set.

When the yoghurt has set, it should be placed in the refrigerator or a cool place until eaten. The yoghurt incubated in a vacuum flask should at this stage be poured into another container. You can make your own fruit yoghurt by stirring in fruit or jam after it has set, or sweeten it to taste by adding sugar.

If you use a bought yoghurt as the initial culture it is wise to buy a new one each time you make yoghurt. Contamination could occur if a portion of the home-made yoghurt is saved to act as a 'starter' for the next batch. Making yoghurt at home is still inexpensive, since a small carton of yoghurt can be used to make a large amount of fresh yoghurt. If you use a yoghurt culture, this can be recultivated and maintained in the same way as described for cheese starter (pages 29–36), but remember to incubate it at 110°F (43°C).

CREAM

Cream contains most of the milk fat together with a proportion of the other milk constituents. It is produced from whole milk by separation; the fat which consists of many tiny fat globules is lighter than the rest of the milk, and so the cream rises naturally to the surface. The amount of

71

cream in the milk, and its colour, depend largely on the breed of cow; milk from the Channel Island breeds and South Devon cows has a high fat content and the cream is a rich yellow colour.

Commercial dairies separate cream by centrifugal force in a mechanical separator. Creams of varying butterfat content can be produced by this process and those available on the market include:

Half cream (minimum fat content 12 per cent) This may be called 'top of the milk' and is a pouring cream.

Single cream (18 per cent) A pouring cream ideal for coffee, soup and desserts. It will not whip as the fat content is too low.

Sterilized cream (23 per cent) A thicker cream with a slight caramel flavour; available in cans. As it has been sterilized it should keep for up to two years if unopened.

Whipping cream (35 per cent) The best cream for whipping; it should whip up to twice its volume.

Double cream (48 per cent) A rich pouring cream; it will whip but better results are obtained if a tablespoon of milk is added to each $\frac{1}{4}$ pint of cream. There is also a 'thick' double cream which is heavily homogenized and will not whip.

Clotted cream (55 per cent) A thick cream with its own special 'nutty' flavour and golden yellow colour. It is made by a process of scalding the cream (described page 74) and is produced chiefly in the West Country.

Producing cream at home

If you have a ready supply of raw milk you may like to separate your own cream. You will need a large shallow pan and a hand skimmer (illustration 22) (see list in appendix for suppliers). If you cannot obtain the skimmer a thin-edged saucer can be used. Pour the warm milk, fresh from the cow, into the pan and leave it to stand for 24 hours in a cool place, so that the fat comes to the surface and forms a thin layer of cream. If you are using goat's milk you will have to leave it for longer since the fat globules are smaller than those in cow's milk, and the cream consequently takes longer to rise. Do not leave any strong smelling substance near the milk as cream readily absorbs flavours.

Now skim the cream using a sharp-edged perforated skimmer, which allows the skimmed milk to drain back into the pan. Start by breaking it off at the pan edges – it will peel back like a thick skin. There will be a

22 *Cream pan and skimmer*

great deal of variation in the consistency of the cream produced by this method, and some of the fat will be left in the skimmed milk. However you will gradually become more expert. The cream you obtain this way should have a butterfat content of about 50 per cent – similar to double cream. If you require a thinner cream, for example to make single cream cheese, you can dilute the cream with an equal quantity of skimmed milk.

Pasteurization of home-produced cream

It is advisable to pasteurize home-produced cream to make sure it is safe and free from contaminating organisms. Pour the cream into a bucket and place this in a larger container filled with boiling water. Raise the temperature of the cream to 145°F (63°C), and hold it at this temperature for 30 minutes. Stir frequently to ensure even heating. Then cool at once to 40°F (4.5°C) by putting the bucket of cream into cold running water.

How to whip cream

It is important that the cream is aged and cooled before it is whipped. During the pasteurization the fat melts, and so aging for at least 24 hours at 40°F (4.5°C) is essential to allow most of the fat to resolidify. This also applies to bought cream; it is advisable to age this first before whipping it because it may have become warm on the journey home from the shops or on the doorstep! After aging you will notice that the cream is thicker.

The cream, whisk and bowl should be really cold. The equipment can be cooled in cold water, or left in the refrigerator for a time before whipping. A hand balloon whisk will give the best results.

Whip the cream quickly at first until it takes on a matt finish, and then slowly until it stands in peaks. Great care should be taken not to overwhip as this will turn the cream into butter!

Making clotted cream

The simplest method is to scald the cream in a double saucepan (or a bowl in a saucepan of boiling water). Heat the cream to 170°–190°F (77°–88°C) and keep it at this temperature until the top of the cream becomes thick and crusty, with a wrinkled appearance. This may take from $\frac{1}{2}$–1 hour depending on the quantity of cream. The cream should be stirred occasionally at first to ensure even heating. Since the cream is being scalded it does not require prior pasteurization. When it is ready remove the top saucepan or bowl and cool it rapidly by placing it in cold water. Leave it in the refrigerator or a cool place for 24 hours. The clotted cream can then be packed in small glass jars or plastic containers, and should be kept in the refrigerator until eaten within 4–5 days.

If you wish to make your own clotted cream from bought cream, use double cream.

BUTTER

Whereas milk is an emulsion of fat globules in a watery solution, butter is an emulsion of water in solidified fat. It is obtained from cream by churning; the churning action causes the fat globules to merge and form butter granules.

74

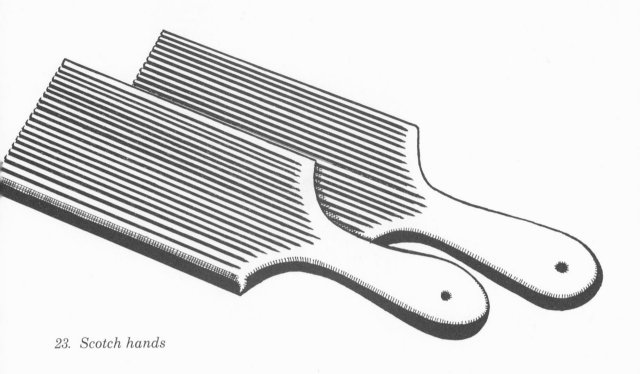

23. Scotch hands

Making butter at home

You can easily make butter at home with an ordinary hand or electric
beater, but there are small hand or electric butter churns available if you
wish to invest in one (see list in appendix for supplier). You will also need
a wooden board, and scotch hands (illustration 23) to work the butter.

First separate your cream and keep it cool until ready for use. You
can use either fresh cream, or ripened cream which is slightly sour.
Ripened cream does give better results. If you are making cheese you will
have cheese starter available and can use this to ripen the cream; alternatively you can obtain special butter starter. Add about 5 fl. oz of starter
to each gallon of cream and leave it in a warm place or incubator – about
70°F (21°C) – for 12 hours (see the section on starter cultivation pages
33–5). After ripening, cool the cream to 40°–45°F (4.5°–7°C) for several
hours to allow the fat to harden again before churning.

The churning temperature is most important – it should be between
50° and 65°F (10°–18°C) depending on the season of the year: lower in hot

summer weather and higher in cooler weather. Bring your cream to the correct temperature. The mixing bowl or churn jar can be stood in a larger bowl of cold or warm water as necessary to obtain the correct temperature. The wooden board and scotch hands should be stood in cold water until used.

Pour the cream into the bowl or churn (illustration 24), filling it not more than half full. You can add a few drops of butter annatto colouring if you wish. Now whisk or churn the cream until it thickens and begins to separate into butter grains and buttermilk; if you use an electric beater, set it at a slow speed. At this stage add some cold water – about 50°F (10°C) – and churn again. This is known as the 'breaking' water and helps to separate and round off the butter grains. If necessary add some more cold water to help the cream to 'break', but the total breaking water used should not amount to more than a quarter of the quantity of cream. Churn until the granules reach the size of wheat grains.

Pour off the buttermilk and save this. Pour cold water over the butter grains to wash them; again the water should be colder than the churning temperature. Whisk or churn for a few seconds, and then run off the water. Repeat the washings until the water runs off as a clear liquid; it is important that all the buttermilk is washed out of the butter, otherwise the butter will not keep and may go rancid.

Collect the butter from the bowl or jar by straining it through a muslin cloth. Press out the water, and if the butter is soft leave it in a cool place to harden a little.

The butter must now be well worked to remove as much water as possible, so that it will keep. Place the butter on a wooden board and pat it with the scotch hands or other suitable utensils to press out the water. Pat it down into a thin layer, fold it over and pat down again. If you slope the board slightly the water can run off. Try to keep the butter as cool as possible. Salt can be worked into the butter at the same time, at the rate of 1–2 teaspoons to each lb of butter, according to taste. Finally pat the butter into shape and wrap it in greaseproof paper. Keep it in the refrigerator or a cool place.

The utensils used in buttermaking should be rinsed, washed and sterilized as before; wooden equipment, however, should be washed in washing soda crystals only since detergent makes the wood sticky and could taint the butter.

If you wish to make your own butter from bought cream you can use whipping or double cream, but it will be fairly expensive butter!

24. *Small hand butter churn*

Buttermilk

The buttermilk contains most of the other milk constituents in a diluted form, and so has some food value; it would be a waste to throw it away. It is a very refreshing drink when cold, and can be used in baking. If you have used ripened cream for buttermaking, the buttermilk will contain some of the culture. You can make your own cultured buttermilk by leaving this in a warm place or incubator – 70°F (21°C) – to coagulate and thicken.

The cultured buttermilk that is available commercially used to be made from buttermilk, but now most of it is made from skimmed milk. A bacterial culture is added and the milk incubated until the desired acidity is reached.

POSTSCRIPT

By now you will be familiar with many of the cheesemaking processes and will perhaps already have discovered that it is a relatively easy craft – once you have collected together your equipment, mastered a few techniques such as sterilization and the recultivation of starter, and experimented a few times.

Indeed experimentation and improvisation may be the key to your own cheesemaking. The recipes and methods given in this book have worked well for me, but there is no reason why, having mastered the basic principles, you should not experiment to find your own recipes both for soft and hard cheeses. Indeed you will soon find that no two cheeses turn out exactly the same even if you do follow the same recipe. Half the fun of cheesemaking is not knowing exactly how successful you have been until you sit down to taste your finished cheese.

The equipment suggested is simple and works well for small amounts of milk, but you may be able to improvise bigger and better equipment if you are dealing with larger milk quantities.

Whatever sort of cheese you are making its nutritional value will be high. So in making cheese you are not only enjoying a fascinating craft, but are producing an essential and extremely satisfying commodity for yourself and your family.

Susan Ogilvy
1976

Appendix

GLOSSARY

You may be unfamiliar with some of the terms used in the book. Here they are listed alphabetically with a simple explanation of their meaning *in the context of this book*, and a page reference to where further details can be found in the text.

Acid curd   Formed by the action of a relatively high acidity on the milk protein; the protein separates and a curd is formed in which the liquid whey is held (compare with rennet curd). *pp. 11, 15*

Acidity   The amount of acid in the milk, the milk's sourness. Acidity is very important in the cheesemaking process and is produced by the lactic-acid bacteria present in the milk. *pp. 10–12*

Aging cream   Keeping cream at a cold temperature – 40°F (4.5°C) – for at least 24 hours. During pasteurization the fat in the cream melts and aging is necessary to resolidify it, and so ensure good results when whipping it. *p. 74*

Annatto   A natural vegetable extract used to give a reddish or orange colour to cheese or butter. *p. 28*

Antibiotic   A substance capable of destroying micro-organisms. *p. 37*

Bacteria   Microscopic unicellular organisms found almost everywhere; some types are beneficial – for example the cheesemaking bacteria – and some are harmful and cause disease. *pp. 11, 13, 16*

Calcium   A mineral element, greyish white in colour; a major constituent of bones and teeth. Milk and cheese are rich sources of calcium in our diet and owe their white colour to its presence. *p. 10*

Casein   A milk protein which has the ability to precipitate when rennet is added or the milk becomes very acid. *p. 10*

Cheese starter   A special bacterial culture used to produce acid during cheesemaking and to contribute to the flavour of the cheese. The bacteria use the milk sugar, lactose, for growth and change it to lactic acid. *pp.11, 14*

Emulsion   A watery liquid with oily or fatty particles suspended in it. *p. 74*

Enzymes   Naturally occurring chemical compounds which help bring about chemical changes. *p.13*

Freeze-dried culture   A culture which has been frozen and then heated in a vacuum so that the ice formed on freezing evaporates directly as vapour without turning back into moisture. It is reactivated when added to liquid milk. *p.37*

Homogenization   A process in which the fat globules in milk and cream are broken down to smaller particles and evenly distributed so that the fat does not rise to the surface.

Incubation   The provision of a constant warm temperature to allow the bacterial culture to grow. *pp. 33–5*

Junket   A semi-solid curd formed when rennet is added to warm milk. *p.10*

Lactose   The milk sugar; it can be changed to lactic acid by certain bacteria, thereby increasing the acidity of the milk. *p.10*

Moulds   Minute fungi which exhibit a woolly or furry growth. *pp.14–15*

Pasteurization   A mild heat treatment – the milk is heated to 160°F (71°C) for 15 seconds and then cooled rapidly. This kills all disease organisms and most lactic acid-producing bacteria. *pp. 11, 15, 26–7*

Proteins   Organic compounds which form an important part of all living organisms; they are essential constituents of the diet of animals. *pp. 10–11*

Rennet   A substance containing rennin and other enzymes which is found in the stomach of young mammals and has the property of clotting milk. *p.10*

Rennet curd   The curd formed when rennet is added to milk (compare with acid curd). *p.11*

Sterilized milk   Milk which has been homogenized, then heat-treated to above boiling point – not less than 212°F (100°C) for 20–30 minutes. This process destroys bacteria and other micro-organisms more completely than pasteurization. The heat treatment gives the milk a creamy colour and a slight caramel flavour; sterilized milk is sold in long slender bottles with crown caps. *p. 10*

Sterilization   The destruction of all micro-organisms by heat or chemical means. *p. 25*

Topstir   Stir the top quarter-inch of milk very firmly and smoothly after the addition of rennet until coagulation takes place. This prevents the fat from rising to the surface. *p.44*

Ultra-heat-treated milk   Milk which is heated to very high temperature for a very short time – 270°F (132°C) for one second. This heat treatment sterilizes the milk but does not affect its taste and colour. Aseptically packed in aluminium foil packs, it keeps for several months if unopened. Known as 'long-life milk'. *pp. 10, 26, 70*

Whey   The liquid produced when milk clots. It is held in the curd and released gradually when the curd is cut, heated, drained or pressed. Consists mostly of water and lactose together with a small proportion of other milk constituents. *p. 10*

Yoghurt   A cultured milk product produced by the growth of 'yoghurt' lactic-acid bacteria; an acid curd is formed. *p. 69*

SOME AMERICAN SOURCES OF STARTER CULTURES*

The Dairy Laboratories, 2300 Locust Street, Philadelphia, Pennsylvania
Chris Hansen's Laboratory, 9015 West Maple Street, Milwaukee, Wisconsin
Klenzade Products Company, Beloit, Wisconsin
Marschall Dairy Laboratory, P.O. Box 592, Madison, Wisconsin
Meyer-Blanke Company, St. Louis, Missouri
W. K. Mosely Laboratory, Indianapolis, Indiana
Albert Verley and Company, 1375 East Linden Avenue, Linden, New Jersey
Ziegler and Son, Topeka, Kansas
Dairy Products Laboratories, San Francisco, California
Dairy Technics, Kalamazoo, Michigan
American Type Culture Collection, 12301 Parklawn Drive, Rockville, Maryland

Chris Hansen's Laboratory and some of the other firms listed above should be able to supply the American reader with a variety of starter cultures for different cheeses and yoghurt, as well as ingredients such as rennet and annatto. Dairy Technics specializes in frozen starter concentrates. Inquiries regarding prices and instructions for the use of various culture forms should be addressed to the laboratory.
For a complete catalog of cheesemaking equipment and accessories, presses, molds, thermometers, and so on, also information about a complete brick cheese kit capable of producing semi-soft cheeses complete with mold dairy thermometer and all accessories, write to:
   Homecraft, 111 Stratford Center, Winston-Salem, North Carolina 27104

A specially designed hardwood cheese press with two molds can be obtained from:
   Al Ewing, P.O. Box 197, Ridgeway, Colorado 81432
Mr Ewing intends to expand his stock of cheesemaking equipment in the near future and interested readers should request his catalog.

* Courtesy of Dr Frank V. Kosikowski of Cornell University, from his book *Cheese and Fermented Milk Foods*.

SUPPLIERS OF EQUIPMENT
AND INGREDIENTS

Before ordering your equipment and ingredients it is advisable to send for a
catalogue and current price list.

Dairy thermometers	J. J. Blow Ltd, Oldfield Works, Chatsworth Rd, Chesterfield, s40 2DJ
	Astell Laboratory Service Company, 172, Brownhill Rd, Catford, London, SE6 2DL
	Richard List, Godington, Bicester, Oxon, OX6 9AF
	Clares Carlton Ltd, Wells, Somerset, BA5 1SQ
Stainless steel mixing bowls	J. J. Blow Ltd
Stainless steel buckets	J. J. Blow Ltd
	Coldstream (Engineering) Ltd, 12, Fellbrigg Rd, East Dulwich, London, SE22 9HH
Dairythene plastic bucket	J. J. Blow Ltd
Coulommiers cheese moulds	Clares Carlton Ltd
4 oz polythene starter bottles with caps	Astell Laboratory Service Company
Equipment for 'Lewis' method of starter cultivation (including polythene bottles, rubber seals, inoculation needle unit)	Astell Laboratory Service Company
Small hard cheese mould with follower	Richard List
Cream setting pan	J. J. Blow Ltd
Cream skimmer	J. J. Blow Ltd
	Richard List
Butter churns – hand and electric	J. J. Blow Ltd
Butter churns – hand	Richard List

0749.
Wells 73900

83

Cheese rennet	Clares Carlton Ltd
	R. J. Fullwood and Bland Ltd, Ellesmere, Salop, SY12 9DG
Annatto – cheese colour and butter colour	Chr. Hansen's Laboratory Ltd, 476, Basingstoke Rd, Reading RG2 0QL
Junket tablets	R. J. Fullwood and Bland Ltd

Cheese starter
    Liquid cultures   R. J. Fullwood and Bland Ltd

                                Chr. Hansen's Laboratory Ltd

                                Enolacto Ltd, 8 Hillfield Court, London, NW3

                                West of Scotland Agricultural College, Dept of Dairy Technology, Auchincruive, Ayr, KA6 5HW

                                Somerset College of Agriculture and Horticulture, Cannington, near Bridgwater, TA5 2LS

    Freeze-dried cultures   Chr. Hansen's Laboratory Ltd

                                  Enolacto Ltd

                                  West of Scotland Agricultural College

Yoghurt culture
    Liquid and freeze-dried cultures   Chr. Hansen's Laboratory Ltd

                                  Enolacto Ltd

                                  West of Scotland Agricultural College

Butter starter   Chr. Hansen's Laboratory Ltd

                                  Enolacto Ltd

                                  West of Scotland Agricultural College

FURTHER READING

André Simon, *Cheeses of the World,* Faber, 1956, 2nd edition 1960

Val Cheke, *The Story of Cheesemaking in Britain*, Routledge and Kegan Paul, 1959

V. Cheke and A. Sheppard, *Cheese and Butter,* Rupert Hart-Davies

J. G. Davis, *Cheese* (in two volumes), J. A. Churchill, 1965

J. G. Davis, *Dictionary of Dairying*, Leonard Hill, 1965

T. A. Layton, *Cheese and Cheese Cookery*, Wine and Food Society Publishing Company

Bee Nilson, *Cooking with Yoghurt, Cultured Cream and Soft Cheese.* Pelham Books, 1973

Various advisory leaflets issued by the Ministry of Agriculture, Fisheries and Food:

Soft Cheese, no. 458, revised 1975

Cream Cheese, no. 222, revised 1973

Starters for Cheesemaking, no. 302, 1962

Cream, no. 495, revised 1971

Clotted Cream, no. 438, revised 1971

Also:

Dairy Work for Goatkeepers, published by the British Goat Society, Rougham, Bury St Edmunds, Suffolk, IP30 9LJ

The US Department of Agriculture also publishes a booklet, *Cheese Varieties and Descriptions* (Handbook no. 54).

METRIC CONVERSION

We have used imperial units in this book on the grounds that most people are more familiar with them and will continue to use them, at least for the time being. For those, however, who wish to use metric measurements, the following guidelines will help with the conversion. (Note that these are *not* direct conversion figures; they have been rounded up or down, and are only relevant for use in this book.)

Capacity Volumes of liquid are measured in litres (l.) and millilitres (ml). 1 fluid ounce (fl. oz) is approximately equal to 30 ml; 2 fl. oz = 60 ml, and so on. For measuring small quantities, teaspoons and tablespoons can be replaced by ml measuring spoons as follows:

$\frac{1}{4}$ teaspoon = 1.25 ml spoon
$\frac{1}{2}$ teaspoon = 2.5 ml spoon
1 teaspoon = 5 ml spoon
1 tablespoon = 15 ml spoon

1 tablespoon or 15 ml spoon holds $\frac{1}{2}$ fl. oz; 2 tablespoons or 2 × 15 ml spoons hold 1 fl. oz.

Metric cookery Recipes can be based on a 25 gramme (g.) unit as the equivalent of one ounce. Thus 2 oz is equivalent to 50 g., 3 oz to 75 g. and so on. The ingredient proportions will remain the same if you use the same number of eggs as stated in the original recipe and 60 ml instead of $\frac{1}{8}$ pint milk. The metric recipe will make up to a slightly smaller quantity, so cooking times should be slightly shorter using the stated oven temperatures. For example, where a 30-minute cooking time is stated, 25 minutes should be adequate.

Conversion notes on individual methods and recipes   *Sterilization*   P. 25 Dilution of hypochlorite – use 30 ml (1 fl. oz) in 4.5 l. (1 gallon) water.

Soft cheeses: lemon, buttermilk, yoghurt, lactic, Crowdie, whey cheeses For 1 pint use 500 ml of milk which will make about 100–125 g. soft cheese; for 2 pints use 1 l.
Coulommiers and Colwick For 1 gallon of milk use 4.5 l.; for $\frac{1}{2}$ oz salt use 15 g.
Cambridge For 1$\frac{1}{2}$ gallons use 7 l. of milk which will make 2 cheeses of 350–450 g. each. For the coloured stripe remove 2 l. from each 7 l. of milk.
Cream cheese For 1 pint of cream use 500 ml; for pressing use $\frac{1}{2}$–1 kilogramme (kg) weights; add 6 g. salt.
Mysost 1 l. of whey will make about a 100 g. cheese.

Semi-hard cheese For 2 gallons use 9 l. of milk which will make about a 900 g. cheese.
Smallholder cheese Use 20 g. salt to 9 l. of milk. Put on initial weights up to 13 kg and then after turning up to 18 kg. For finishing use 30–60 g. lard.
Caerphilly Add 25 g. salt to each 1,500 g. curd. Use 2 kg weights for pressing.
Cheshire Add 25 g. to each 1,100 g. curd. Use 4 kg weights for pressing.

Yoghurt For 1 pint of milk use 500 ml.

86 *Butter* Use 125 ml starter for each 4 l. cream. Add 1–2 ml of salt to each 500 g. butter.

Index

The numbers in *italics* refer to the figure numbers of the illustrations